KNOW YOUR

FAITH

All Basic Catholic Beliefs

————•————

*With a Summary of
Chief Vatican II Messages*

**Prepared for
Adult and Youthful Catholics**

**By
FATHER RAYMOND B. FULLAM, S.J.**
S.T.L., M.ED.

Illustrated

CATHOLIC BOOK PUBLISHING CORP.
New York

NIHIL OBSTAT: Michael J. Wrenn, M.A., M.S.
Censor Librorum

IMPRIMATUR: ✠ Joseph T. O'Keefe, D.D.
Vicar General, Archdiocese of New York

This book is in accord with the newly revised Canon Law of the Catholic Church.

(T-259)

ISBN 978-0-89942-259-6

INTRODUCTION

Dear Adult or Youthful Reader:

ABOVE all, this book is intended to help reassure those adults who may have become somewhat unsure about just what the Catholic Church teaches these days.

While a professor of Theology develops religious nuances of a topic, the College and Seminary young men and women might well use this small compendium of Catholic doctrine to focus in on precisely what the Church holds and teaches while the students scan the horizons for religious truths today.

In either Sophomore or Junior years, High School youth are eager to learn clear Catholic teachings on doctrine, morality, and worship. Hence, this book would be most suitable for these times.

And since 8th grade is a fine opportunity to pull together all Catholic topics, this is a good time to employ this book. Certainly, for those preparing to receive the Sacrament of Responsibility, "Knowing Your Faith" would be excellent for preparing for the outpouring of the Holy Spirit in Confirmation C.C.D. classes today.

All might memorize the chief religious definitions in the dark print for future use and for quick recall when consolation is needed.

Experienced teachers of religion will now know what to assign to be memorized by their students, when to stress certain important ideas, and how to help their students toward living the precious truths of our Catholic faith.

In addition to the doctrinal presentation within the chapters, the appendices include Useful Questions for Each Chapter, a Summary of Chief Vatican II Messages, and Basic Catholic Prayers—all of which should prove interesting, useful, and profitable.

I would like to address a word to all readers at this point. In order to absorb the basics of our Catholic beliefs contained in "Knowing Your Faith," let the subject seep deeply into your mind and heart by reading it all very slowly, even prayerfully, so that these religious truths will become your very own—something first understood.

Finally, may the befriending Holy Spirit of God enlighten your mind and inflame your soul so you enjoy the basics of our Catholic beliefs which are contained in "Knowing Your Faith."

With many blessings to you,

Father Raymond B. Fullam, S.J.

CONTENTS

8 CONTENTS

PART ONE
Our Creed of Catholic Teachings

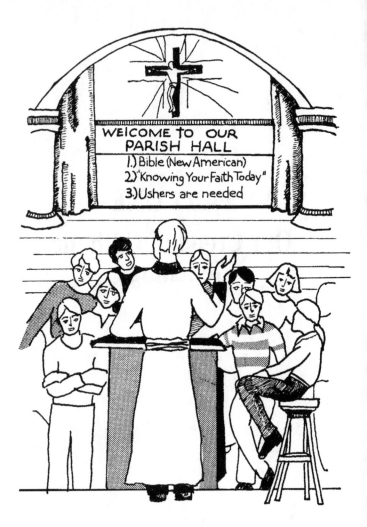

WELCOME TO OUR
PARISH HALL
1.) Bible (New American)
2.) "Knowing Your Faith Today"
3.) Ushers are needed

*To stay spiritually alive is to deepen
your Catholic Teachings.*

PART ONE

OUR CREED OF CATHOLIC TEACHINGS

RELIGIOUS truths should not only continually grow in our minds but also especially blossom in the very fiber of our inner beings.

By nurturing what is true and good and helpful we thereby strengthen the roots of our faith.

Since you are a baptized Catholic, you already have much good potential in your favor. After all, along with being baptized, you have within you God's tremendously helpful, supernatural graces of infused faith, and hope, and charity. You also have the very mark of Jesus Christ on your soul. And He will surely pour on you His many helping or actual graces every day. All you have to do is to try to listen to those little good whisperings **into your mind from the Lord and cooperate with His promptings** for your will to do good or avoid evil.

But much will depend on how deeply you have taken in Our Creed of Catholic Teachings and how much these saving truths really mean to you in practice.

Also, you can mostly respond to God's goodness to you by knowing your faith and striving to live it well. It is well worth the effort to learn what a true Catholic fully believes and practices!

Before this book becomes published, it will have to bear the Bishop's approval, his "Imprimatur," which means "let it be printed." This appears on the other side of the title page. So you can feel safe and sure while reading and absorbing the contents of Our Creed of Catholic teachings.

Our relationship with God can be alive with eternal life.

I.
WHAT RELIGION IS

The Importance of Religion

1. What should be the relationship between human beings and God?

The relationship between human beings and God is that of the creature to the Creator. This imposes on human beings the duties and obligations of knowledge, love, and obedience.

2. How can persons attain eternal salvation?

By knowing, loving, and obeying God in this life, human beings can gain the eternal salvation of their soul.

The salvation of the soul consists in the everlasting happiness of a human as an intelligent being; it encompasses the complete satisfaction of the highest powers of the soul, namely the intellect and the will in an everlasting union with God and loved ones in heaven.

(For useful questions on the above chapter, see p. 141.)

Christ's love opens the doors of His love
making our lives fruitful and bright.

II.
GOD REVEALS SAVING TRUTHS TO US

What Revelation Is All About

3. Why must we believe what God has revealed?

We must believe what God has revealed because God cannot err or lead us into error.

"To reveal" means to show or explain. Divine revelation pertains to God's showing mankind His way to salvation.

And this revelation is contained in the Bible and in Sacred Tradition.

Oral tradition, a handing on by word of mouth, came before the written New Testament. Christ and His Apostles spoke the word of God in public discourse and informally with individuals and groups. There were Christians before any book of the New Testament was written.

The Holy Bible in Itself

4. Why is the Bible considered as divinely inspired?

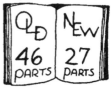

The Bible is a collection of 73 sacred books, which were composed under the positive influence of the Holy Spirit by men chosen by God and which have been accepted by the Church as divinely inspired.

The Bible is the most authorized, the most admirable, and the most important book in the world because it is the only "divine" book, the word of God in the language of man.

The Bible is composed of 73 inspired books (it is really a library of holy books) written over the course of 1,000 years, from about 950 B.C. to 100 A.D.

Other names for the Bible are: Holy or Sacred Scripture(s), Holy Writ, the Sacred Writings, the Good Book, and the Word of God.

The two main parts of the Bible are the Old Testament and the New Testament.

5. In relation to the Bible what does "testament" mean?

The word "testament" is here used in the sense of "agreement" or "covenant." The Old Testament is a record of the old agreement between God (Yahweh) and His chosen people, the Hebrews. It portrays the remote preparation for the coming of the Messiah and the founding of His Church.

6. What is the New Testament?

The New Testament is a record of the new agreement made by God with the whole human race through the Life, Death, and Resurrection of Jesus Christ, the Son of God made Man. It establishes the start and the promises of Christ's Church.

The principal author of the Bible is God.

God revealed Himself in time. He intervened in history and communicated to human beings His merciful plans for their salvation. The Bible (the

Word of God) is the record of this self-revelation of God which was set forth in a message as well as in events. God spoke and acted—word and event went together.

Divine Inspiration of the Bible

7. What is the inspiration of the Bible?

The inspiration of the Bible is a divine action or supernatural influence of the Holy Spirit on the sacred writers.

This influence moved and impelled them to write in such a manner that they first understood rightly, then willed faithfully to write down, and fully expressed in apt words and with infallible truth all the things, and those only, which God had designed.

8. What is biblical inerrancy?

Biblical inerrancy is the quality flowing from the inspiration of the Holy Spirit by which the Scriptures—both in theory and in fact—are free from all error in the messages they intend to convey.

The sacred writers made use of customary linguistic wording then in practice.

What "Gospel" Means

The word Gospel means "good news," the great glad tidings of available salvation proclaimed by Christ and His Church today. Gospel also refers to the four forms in which this good news has come down to us in written form: Matthew, Mark, Luke, and John.

The first three Gospels are very similar and are called "Synoptic" because their contents can be encompassed right away once they are placed in three columns side by side. In their composition the Evangelists used similar sources. But each author has his own distinctive style and arrangement.

The Gospel Writers

9. What do each of the Gospel writers seek to establish?

The Gospel according to Matthew constantly seeks to bring out the majesty of Jesus as Messiah and Son of God.

The Gospel according to Mark desires to establish a close bond between the Passion of Jesus and His Lordship, showing that the Son of Man had to undergo the Cross before attaining His glory.

The Gospel according to Luke portrays Christianity as a faith or religion open to all human beings regardless of nation or culture. His depiction of Jesus shows the Savior's concern also for the poor, the needy, and the outcasts.

The Gospel according to John is more sublime, mystical, and theological. Some feel it is even more warm. He makes use of signs and reflective discourses to reveal Christ's present mission as Word, Way, Truth, Life, and Light. John's purpose is to inspire belief in Jesus as the Messiah, the Son of God (Jn 20:31).

Our Sacred Church Tradition

10. What does Sacred Church Tradition mean?

Sacred Tradition is the Word of God given to the Apostles by Christ and the Holy Spirit and handed down to their successors through the Church.

This was done by means of prayers and Creeds, liturgical practices, and authoritative writings such as through the Popes, bishops, and theologians.

11. What three sources combine to bring us God's Revelation?

Tradition can be seen as the way the Church understands and lives the teachings of Jesus at any particular time in history. Tradition and Sacred Scripture comprise one deposit of the faith. Consequently, Scripture, Tradition, and the Catholic Church combine to bring us God's Revelation.

Use of the Bible by Catholics

12. How should we read the Bible?

We should read the Bible with the mind of the Church because it is the Church who gave us the Bible and who interprets it for us. Then the Bible will become God's Word to us today.

The Catholic Church is the official interpreter of the Bible. As the people of God—both of the Old Testament in figure and of the New Covenant in reality—the people of the Church wrote the Sacred Scriptures. As the Church of Christ, she is empowered to interpret them for us. As the Church of Christians, she has always treasured God's Holy Word. Certainly, as is done during Mass, we gain much by reading devotedly the Sacred Scriptures.

What God has revealed is taught to us by the Catholic Church. Faith is absolutely necessary for salvation because without faith no one can please God.

Some claim that it does not matter what we believe, as long as we live correctly. Such an attitude is an insult to the Lord. God sent His own divine Son into the world in order to teach us the way to heaven. But if God Himself went to such an extent to teach us what we must believe, it must have been very important to Him that we know and believe His saving truths. Clearly, without faith, without believing what God teaches, we cannot live right—not correctly in the eyes of God.

(For useful questions on the above chapter, see p. 141.)

Our chief act of faith in Christ's Revelations is reflected in the Blessed Trinity's unity.

III.
ONE GOD IN THREE DIVINE PERSONS, THE MOST BLESSED TRINITY

The Apostles' Creed

13. What is the wording of the Apostles' Creed?

The apostles' creed reads as follows:

"I believe in God, the Father Almighty, Creator of heaven and earth. And in Jesus Christ, His only Son, our Lord; Who was conceived by the Holy Spirit, born of the Virgin Mary, suffered under Pontius Pilate, was crucified, died, and was buried. He descended into hell; the third day He rose again from the dead; He ascended into heaven, and sits at the hand of God, the Father Almighty; from thence He shall come again to judge the living and the dead. I believe in the Holy Spirit, the Holy Catholic Church, the Communion of Saints, the forgiveness of sins, the resurrection of the body, and life everlasting. Amen."

This profession of faith is called "The Apostles' Creed" because according to ancient tradition, it goes back to the Apostles themselves.

Who God Is

14. Who is God?

God is the eternal, infinite, all-powerful, all-wise perfect Spirit, Who is Lord of heaven and earth.

"God is Spirit" (Jn 4:24).—"I am God, and there is no other; I am God, and there is none like Me" (Isa 46:9)

That "God is infinitely perfect" means that He possesses every good quality or attribute in the highest degree. He is eternal and unchanging, omnipresent, all-knowing, all-wise, all-powerful, infinitely perfect, holy, and just, infinitely good and merciful, infinitely true and faithful.

God's Existence Proven

15. How do we know for certain that God exists?

We know God exists

a) **from reasoning about the world of things around us,**

b) **from the voice of conscience within us,**

c) **and most clearly from divine Revelation available to us.**

1) Reason tells us that the world did not always exist but must have had a beginning. It could not have made itself. An almighty Creator must have called it into being by some means. Also, within our

world and the universe there exists marvelous order which could not have been the result of mere chance. An all-wise and all-powerful supreme Being must have organized it all. Him we call God.

2) We constantly hear within us the mysterious voice of conscience telling us what is good to do and what is bad. Conscience is not something which people give to themselves. It must have been planted in our hearts by a wise and just judge whom we know as God.

3) Vatican Council II stresses a known fact; "God, the beginning and end of all things, can be known with certainty from created reality by the light of human reason (see Rom 1:20), but . . . it is through God's revelation that those religious truths which are by their nature accessible to human reason can be known by all people with ease, with solid certitude, and with no trace of error, even in the present state of the human race" (Vatican II on Revelation, no. 6).

God's Attributes or Perfections

16. Why is God all-powerful?

"God is all-powerful" means that He can do all things whatever He wills, in whatever manner He wills, and for whomever He wills.

"Nothing will be impossible for God" (Lk 1:37). "The Lord does whatever He pleases in heaven and on earth, in the seas and in all their depths" (Ps 135:6).

"God is just" means that He rewards the good and punishes the wicked, according as each deserves.

"He judges everyone impartially on the basis of each person's deeds" (1 Pet 1:17).

The Most Blessed Trinity

17. Who are the Three Divine Persons in the Most Blessed Trinity?

In God there are three divine Persons: the Father, the Son, and the Holy Spirit. These three divine Persons are only the one God. And we call these three equally divine Persons in the one God the Most Blessed Trinity.

We call God the creator of heaven and earth because it was from nothing that He made heaven, earth, all human souls, and everything.

The first two chapters of Genesis in the Bible recount the creation of the world. The Bible, however, does not intend what we would call a scientific description; its purpose is to teach us that everything which does exist was created by God.

God still watches over our world; He orders and directs everything for the best, drawing some good out of everything.

The Problem of Evil in our World

18. Why does God sometimes allow some sin and evil in our world?

God permits sin and evil in our world

a) because he wants our choice of Him to be free in spite of some sin and evil;

b) and because He can turn even evil, or sin, to some good.

(For useful questions on the above chapter, see p. 142.)

God is the Creator and Master of all

IV.
GOD THE CREATOR OF ANGELS, ALL HUMAN BEINGS, AND EVERYTHING ELSE

The Angels

19. What are Angels?

Angels are spiritual beings, created by God to worship Him, to serve Him, to carry out His commands, to befriend Him, and to watch over us on earth.

Our Lord Himself said, "Take care that you do not despise one of these little ones, for I tell you that their angels in heaven gaze continually on the face of My heavenly Father" (Mt 18:10).

Evil Spirits

20. What are evil spirits?

Evil spirits are fallen angels, become devils, who hate God and try to harm us in body and soul, especially for eternity.

According to Old Testament teaching, Satan or the Devil is a personal power hostile to God (Job 1:6; Zec 3:1; Wis 2:24). In the New Testament there are frequent manifestations of the devil and evil spirits. Even Christ was tempted (Mt 4:1-11). And St. Peter puts us on guard against the devil, *"Remain sober and alert, for your enemy the devil is on the prowl like a roaring lion, looking for someone to devour. Resist him and be firm in your faith"* (1 Pet 5:8-9).

Human Beings

21. What happens when a human being is conceived?

In human conception, when the mother's egg becomes fertilized by the father's sperm, at some time God breathes forth into the developing egg an immortal soul.

This is the beginning of the human person and of his or her principle of life, giving life to this person, all his or her other powers like intellect and will together with all the faculties to see, touch, hear, etc., and destined one day to be in heaven with the Lord of life and with loved ones forever.

(For useful questions on the above chapter, see p. 142.)

Repentance over sin goes beyond falls into the light of Christ's strengthening mercy.

V.
OF SIN, ORIGINAL AND PERSONAL

Our Original Sin Inherited from Adam and Eve

22. What was God's most precious gift to Adam and Eve?

The most precious gift that God bestowed on the first man and woman was the life of His Grace.

The first man and woman, Adam and Eve, lost the life of grace by disobeying God, even after they had been warned.

23. What is meant by the Original Sin with which all people are born?

By original sin all human beings are born in need of God's sanctifying grace before they have been baptized even though they themselves have not actually sinned.

Actual Sin, Personal and
Communal

24. When do human beings personally sin?

We ourselves personally sin when we knowingly, deliberately, and intentionally break a commandment of God or a precept of the Church.

Because of the attraction to commit evil after original sin, we have unfortunately, the potential to personally and communally commit actual sins.

Desire in itself is not sin. It can be evil when the desire is for something bad and it is, nevertheless, given approval by the will. This means consenting to satisfy the bad desire to do something evil.

Not all faults are equally grave. There are some sins of such seriousness that if all three conditions are present, they become mortal. Then there are some things which are less serious, and some of these can be venial sins.

Sacred Scripture compares some sins to a plank in the eye while others are compared to a speck (Mt 7:3).

God begs us not to sin but He does permit us to be tempted in order that we may: (a) prove our faithfulness, (b) stay humble acknowledging our need for constant help, (c) and increase our merits by overcoming temptations.

"Blessed is the man who perseveres when he is tempted, for when he has successfully endured the time of trial, he will receive the crown of life" (Jas 1:12).

Temptation only becomes sin when a person consents to it, like letting it stay by encouraging it.

We are inwardly warned against sinning by our conscience, which prods us to do what is good and avoid what is evil. When we have done something good, conscience happily approves (a clear conscience). If we have done something evil, conscience rightfully accuses (a worried conscience).

The Nature and Kinds of Personal Sin, and the Conditions for It

25. What are the general ways of committing a personal sin?

The ways of sinning, in general, are:

a) **by deliberate bad thoughts, desires, words, or deeds;**

b) **and by neglect or omission of a good that is one's duty**

26. Under what conditions would a person commit a serious sin?

A person commits mortal sin when he or she

a) **has deliberately done a grave evil,**

b) **has understood the gravity of that evil,**

c) **and acts voluntarily in doing such evil.**

For something to be a serious sin, three conditions are necessary.

(1) *Grave matter.* Not all the things that people do and not all duties and responsibilities have the same moral ramifications. A serious matter has to be so grave that it leaves our basic orientation to God badly marred. A lesser matter leaves this basic orientation untouched, as a venial sin.

(2) *Knowledge of the gravity at the time of doing it.* Mortal sin presupposes that a person realizes the moral seriousness of his or her actions. Without this realization the sin is not mortal, but it may be a bad venial sin.

(3) *The bad action must be freely and voluntarily performed.* This means that the person is not under

emotional or physical compulsion but rather must knowingly and wilfully act against the will of God as he or she understands it in this situation.

If there is any doubt about even one of these three conditions, there is no mortal sin in what was done. But if a person deliberately puts himself in dangerous situations he or she is considered culpable of the consequences.

Persons commit venial sins when they have

(1) a lesser matter

(2) or a grave matter but are not sufficiently aware of the gravity of the act or do not give full consent to it.

The Christian life, however, is motivated not by calculation, but love for God. When we truly love God, we will not want to deliberately offend Him even by venial sin.

The Seven Capital Sins

27. What are the names of the seven capital sins?

The seven capital sins are (1) pride, (2) covetousness, (3) lust, (4) envy, (5) gluttony, (6) anger, and (7) sloth.

These are called "capital sins" because each is the source of many other sins.

"Be faithful to the Lord all the days of your life, my son, and never succumb to the desire to sin or to transgress His commandments" (Tob 4:5).

(For useful questions on the above chapter, see p. 142.)

Christ's Light, Word, and Love always help with our redemption

VI.
JESUS CHRIST, TRUE GOD AND TRUE MAN, OUR LORD AND REDEEMER

The Divinity and Humanity of Jesus

28. Who is Jesus Christ?

Jesus Christ is the true Son of God Who became Man for our sake to redeem us.

Human nature is composed of body and soul. The eternal Son of God always had a divine nature. At Bethlehem He was born a human being, with a human body and soul, that is with a human nature also. But in so doing He did not cease to be God. Hence, Christ is God-Man, true God and true man. His two natures, the human and the divine, are inseparably united in the one Person of the Son of God.

29. How do we know that Jesus Christ was the promised Messiah?

We know that Jesus Christ is the promised Messiah because in Him everything was fulfilled which the prophets had foretold of the Redeemer.

"Philip found Nathaniel and said to him, 'We have found the One about Whom Moses in the Law and also the Prophets wrote—Jesus the son of Joseph, from Nazareth' " (Jn 1:45).

30. How did Jesus Christ prove that He was God?

Jesus Christ proved that He was God

(a) by His miracles

(b) and by His prophecies.

Jesus *worked miracles*, that is, works so extraordinary that they could not be done through merely natural powers but only through the almighty power of God. Christ changed water into wine. He fed several thousand with just a few loaves of bread. He calmed the raging sea in an instant merely by His word to it. He healed by His mere word several people of every type, drove out the devil, and raised the dead to life. *"The very works that I am doing, testify on My behalf that the Father has sent Me" (Jn 5:36).*

Jesus *foretold things* such as no human person could have known in advance, for example, the betrayal of Judas, the flight of the Apostles, Peter's denial, the manner of His own death, and the fact of His Resurrection and Ascension.

Christ's Death, Mankind's Redemption

31. For whom did Jesus die?

Jesus suffered, was crucified, and died for all people.

We know that our Lord rose from the dead principally from the testimony of the Apostles, who saw again the risen Christ with their own eyes, spoke with Him, touched Him, and then later on gave their very lives in evidence that they did indeed see Him alive again.

32. What does the Resurrection of Jesus prove to us?

The Resurrection of Jesus proves to us

a) that Jesus is truly the Son of God,

b) and that one day after our death we also shall rise again, in glory thanks to Jesus Christ.

"Destroy this temple, and in three days I will raise it up" (Jn 2:19). "Just as in Adam all die, so all will be brought to life in Christ" (1 Cor 15:22).

On the fortieth day after His resurrection Jesus gloriously ascended into heaven.

Christ's Ascension into heaven should not be pictured as a sort of voyage into outer space. Though a real departure from earth, it was essentially a supernatural event which eludes human experience or expression. The cloud that took Jesus away suggests the hidden presence of the divine Majesty. The angels assured His disciples that Jesus would return to earth again, but the time of this return remains God's secret. For their part, the Apostles were to be witnesses of Christ *"to the ends of earth."*

"And sits at the right hand of God, the Father Almighty," means that, even as man, Jesus participates in the power and glory of the heavenly Father in eternal bliss. On the third day after His death Jesus reunited His soul with His body and rose in glory, resurrected body and soul, from the grave.

The Resurrection of Christ is the greatest and most important event of our Catholic Faith. St. Paul says, *"If Christ has not been raised, then our preaching is useless, and so is your faith" (1 Cor 15:14).*

And His glorious Ascension into heaven is a further confirmation of the astounding, marvelous, unique Resurrection of our Lord Jesus.

Christ's glorious Ascension, Body and Soul united, as He rose up into heaven as the Apostles looked on confirmed in faith and anticipatory hope, should also be for us a further incentive to know our faith well and strive to live it fruitfully.

(For useful questions on the above chapter, see p. 143.)

The Holy Spirit gladly brings us God's fruitful graces.

VII.
THE HOLY SPIRIT AND GOD'S GRACES AND VIRTUES FOR US

The Holy Spirit, Third Person of the Most Blessed Trinity

33. Who is the Holy Spirit?

The Holy Spirit is the Third Person of the Most Blessed Trinity, true God like the Father and the Son.

The Holy Spirit is a complete and distinct Person, not just an attribute of the Father or the Son. He is the love between the Father and the Son, love of such infinite fullness that it constitutes a third divine Person in the one divine nature. The Holy Spirit is also called "Advocate" or "Counselor," of Whom Christ spoke in His last discourse: *"I will ask the Father, and He will give you another Advocate to be with you forever, the Spirit of Truth Whom the world cannot accept because it neither sees Him nor knows Him" (Jn 14:16-17).*

The Holy Spirit descended in the form of fiery tongues (Acts 2:3). The fiery tongues point to a divine presence, not fear-inspiring as on Mount Sinai (Ex 24:17), but rather conveying supernatural illumination and blessedness.

God's Helping or Actual
Graces for Us

34. What is God's grace for us?

God's grace is an inward, supernatural help or gift which He bestows on us for the good of our soul.

There are two principal kinds of grace:
helping or actual grace
and sanctifying or life giving grace.

Helping grace is also called actual or transient grace: actual because it is given for us to perform supernatural acts; transient because it works on the soul in a temporary or passing manner.

Sanctifying grace, on the other hand, remains in the soul to be constantly pleasing in God's sight, unless it is deliberately driven away.

"We are not competent of ourselves to take credit for anything as coming from us. Our competence comes from God" (2 Cor 3:5-6). "It is God Who is at work in you, enabling you both to desire and to act for His chosen purpose" (Phil 2:13).

35. What does God's help-
ing grace incline us to do?

Helping or actual grace inclines God's people to do good deeds and it helps them to perform them by

a) enlightening our minds

b) and encouraging, moving, and strengthening our will to do good things.

36. What basic grace does God give to every human person?

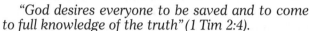

God gives freely to everyone sufficient grace for them to be saved.

"God desires everyone to be saved and to come to full knowledge of the truth" (1 Tim 2:4).

But not everyone receives the same amount of God's grace. A person who cooperates with God's grace will receive more than someone who neglects God and has but little interest in prayer or good works, like seldom or ever going to Mass on weekends when it is now easily available.

Sanctifying Grace, Life of our Soul

37. What does being in sanctifying grace do for us?

Through having sanctifying grace within us, we become holy and in union with God. We also become His children and heirs of heaven.

Sanctifying grace is first received in the Sacrament of Baptism. It removes original sin and its loss of heaven and it sanctifies the soul. Since the baptized person is made holy (just) before God, the sanctifying grace which comes from Baptism is also called the grace of justification.

When it is lost after Baptism, sanctifying grace can again be regained through perfect contrition for that serious sin together with the resolve to go to the priest as soon as an opportunity becomes available.

To preserve and increase sanctifying grace during our lives, we must be devoted to prayer and good works. Good works which can increase sanctifying grace in our souls include: (a) works of piety and penance, (b) works of love of our neighbor, (c) conscientious performance of assigned works in our occupation and elsewhere, and (d) unavoidable suffering borne for love of God and welfare of neighbor. Sacred Scripture also stresses prayer, fasting, and almsgiving. *"It is better to give alms than to hoard gold" (Tob 12:8).*

Especially important are frequent reception of Confession and Holy Communion, because Christ in the Holy Eucharist is the very food which nourishes divine life within our soul.

For our works to be considered as good they should:
conform to the will of God
and be done with a good intention.

(For useful questions on the above chapter, see p. 143.)

*When we reach for Christ's Cross, the Holy Spirit
strengthens us in life's quest for holiness.*

VIII.

OUR AIM IS FOR
HOLINESS OF LIFE

It is not enough to simply avoid sin, however good
that is. We must also grow in virtue and strive for
holiness, even perfection.

The Theological Virtues

38. What are the names of the theological virtues and of the moral virtues?

The chief virtues are classified as

a) the theological virtues which are faith, hope,
and love:

b) and the moral virtues which are prudence,
temperance, justice, and fortitude.

Faith, hope, and charity are called the theological
virtues because along with sanctifying grace they
are infused in the soul by God, and they also refer
directly to God. *"The love of God has been poured
into our hearts through the Holy Spirit that has
been given to us"* (Rom 5:5).

"There are three things that endure: faith, hope, and love, and the greatest of these is love. Pursue love" (1 Cor 13:13, 14:1).

The Moral Virtues

The chief moral virtues are also called "cardinal" or hinge virtues because they regulate our moral life in a manner pleasing to God. PRUDENCE helps us to take definite means to achieve a good end, specifically the best means toward our spiritual good and eternal salvation. TEMPERANCE helps us to master our unruly desires and passions. JUSTICE assists us to render to others whatever is due to them. And FORTITUDE enables us to do what is right even in the face of difficulties, fear, and opposition.

The Seven Gifts of the Holy Spirit are: Wisdom, Understanding, Knowledge, Counsel, Fortitude, Piety, and Fear of the Lord.

The Twelve Fruits of the Holy Spirit are: Charity, Joy, Peace, Patience, Benignity, Goodness, Long-Suffering, Mildness, Faith, Modesty, Continency, and Chastity.

The Beatitudes or Promised Blessings from Christ

39. What is the wording of the eight Beatitudes?

Especially praised in the gospels are the virtues contained in performing the beatitudes (Mt 5:3-11).

1. Blessed are the poor in spirit, for theirs is the kingdom of heaven.

2. Blessed are those who mourn, for they will be comforted.

3. Blessed are the meek, for they will inherit the earth.

4. Blessed are those who hunger and thirst for justice, for they will have their fill.

5. Blessed are the merciful, for they will obtain mercy.

6. Blessed are the pure of heart, for they will see God.

7. Blessed are the peacemakers, for they will be called children of God.

8. Blessed are those who are persecuted in the cause of justice, for theirs is the kingdom of heaven.

The Spiritual and Corporal works of Mercy are also replete with the Lord's blessings. (These are found on pp. 68-69.)

Our Own Imitation of Jesus During Life

40. What is the best way to Christian perfection?

The best way to Christian perfection is to imitate Jesus Christ.

"I am the light of the world. No one who follows Me will ever walk in darkness. Rather, he will have the light of life" (Jn 8:12).

In addition to adoring Jesus in the Most Holy Eucharist, many millions of Catholics have gained hopeful confidence from ardent devotion to the Sacred Heart of Jesus. Many devotees of the Sacred Heart of Jesus start their day by dedicating all their prayers, works, joys, and sufferings of that day to Jesus for the redemption of this world and the Pope's monthly intention.

(For the Morning Offering prayers, see p. 156.)

THE HOLY ROSARY

Another way to imitate Christ is to pray the Holy Rosary, meditating on the principal Mysteries of Christ's life on earth.

The 5 Joyful Mysteries

1. The Annunciation of an Angel to Our Blessed Mother.
2. The Visitation of Our Lady to Her Cousin Elizabeth.
3. The Birth of Jesus in a Stable.
4. The Presentation of Our Lord in the Temple.
5. The Finding of Our Lord in the Temple.

The 5 Luminous Mysteries

1. The Baptism of Jesus in the Jordan.
2. Christ's Self-Manifestation at Cana.
3. Christ's Proclamation of God's Kingdom.
4. The Transfiguration of the Lord.
5. Christ's Institution of the Eucharist.

The 5 Sorrowful Mysteries

1. The Agony in the Garden.
2. The Scourging at the Pillar.
3. The Crowning with Thorns.
4. The Carrying of the Cross.
5. The Crucifixion and Death of Jesus.

The 5 Glorious Mysteries

1. The Resurrection of Our Lord from the Dead.
2. The Ascension of Our Lord into Heaven.
3. The Descent of the Holy Spirit on the Apostles.
4. The Assumption of Our Lady into Heaven.
5. The Crowning of Our Lady as Queen of Heaven.

The Rosary is said by reciting one Our Father followed by 10 Hail Marys and concluding with one Glory be to the Father for each Mystery.

41. What are some chief means for attaining Christian perfection?

Some chief means for attaining Christian perfection are:

a) to want to pray, to be eager for the word of God, and to be devoted to receiving the Sacraments;

b) to practice self-denial and strive to overcome even venial sins;

c) and to be kind to neighbors while striving to perform daily work well while always striving to maintain the state of grace and keep a good intention uppermost.

"Anyone who wishes to follow Me must deny himself, take up his cross daily, and follow Me" (Lk 9:23).

To practice self-denial means to do without some things which are liked, even things that are permitted, so that what is forbidden can more readily be rejected.

Life as a Diocesan or Religious Priest, Sister, or Brother

42. What is the meaning of the three Evangelical Counsels?

The special means of acquiring Christian perfection are contained in the practice of the Evangelical Counsels, which are (a) voluntary poverty, (b) perpetual virginal chastity, and (c) complete obedience.

The Evangelical Counsels are usually assumed under vows in a Religious Congregation after the period of testing known as postulancy or novitiate.

In addition to priests in the Religious Life, Diocesan priests are also bound to keep perpetual chastity and obedience if not by vow then at least by a sacred promise to God through their bishop. They also strive to maintain at least the spirit of the Counsel of poverty. Those in Religious Life take vows to observe all three Counsels.

(For useful questions on the above chapter, see p. 143.)

Though many we are united in our Catholic faith . . .

IX.
OUR CATHOLIC CHURCH

**Founded by Jesus Christ,
Our Lord, Himself**

43. How did God prepare for the founding of Christ's Church?

Before Christ came on earth, God chose Abraham and his descendants as His people thereby preparing for the founding of His Son's Church.

The word "church" stems from the Hebrew word "kahal" (in Greek "kyriakon") meaning house of the Lord, the building and by extension the family or people of God.

44. Basically, what is the Catholic Church?

Basically, the Catholic Church is (a) the mystical body of Christ; (b) the visible kingdom of Christ on earth; (c) with a pope, bishops, priests, and the laity; and (d) the people of God—and all four are aspects of one and the same Church of Christ.

The Pope as Successor of
St. Peter and Visible Head
of the Church on Earth

45. What did Jesus select Peter and his successors to become?

Jesus gathered disciples around Him, chose twelve to be His Apostles, and selected Peter, one of them, as His Vicar or representative on earth. We call his successors our Pope.

Christ promised that Peter would be visible head of the Church in Matthew 16:18-19; then He conferred this office on Peter in John 21:15-17 when Jesus told Peter, *"Feed My lambs, feed My sheep."* Jesus remains the invisible head of His Church as St. Paul says of Christ, *"He is the Head of the body, that is, the Church" (Col 1:18).* But the Church is also a visible community of religious society which cannot endure without a visible head.

Church Government

46. What together are the Pope's administrative bodies called?

The administrative bodies which the Pope uses to help him in governing the Church comprise what is known as "The Vatican Curia."

Formerly, the Pope was also the temporal ruler of the Papal States.

Of rather recent origin is the auxiliary body called Synod of Bishops, which was established by Pope Paul VI on September 15, 1965, at the beginning of the Fourth Session of the Second Vatican Council. This Synod of Bishops meets in Rome with the Pope every three years, as an expression of "Collegiality" established by Vatican II.

47. What is a General Council of the Catholic Church?

A General Council, such as Vatican II was, is an assembly of all the bishops of the world, called together by and presided over by the Pope or his official representatives

Only the Pope can convene a General Council over which he presides and determines the topics to be considered and the parliamentary procedure to be observed; then it is he who declares that Council ended.

When Pope John XXIII died after having begun Vatican Council II, this Council was reconvened by Paul VI, the newly elected Pope. Later, our present Pope John Paul II took the combination of their two names as his own, so devoted was he to those former Popes who had established Vatican II.

Besides bishops, heads of religious orders (abbots-primate etc.) can be invited to attend a General Council as can also some lay people known as "periti," experts in their field, as advisors to their bishops but they do not have the right to vote. Also, women and non-Catholics may be granted admission as observers, as they were during Vatican II.

(For more on Vatican Council II, see appendix B, p. 150.)

48. What is an Encyclical?

When a Pope addresses himself in writing to the whole Catholic world, usually he deals with important matters of faith and morals or he may expound and interpret the Catholic position as regards prevailing trends of thought in the world. These are usually known as "Encyclicals."

Our Bishops and Priests

49. What is a Bishop?

A Bishop is a successor of the Apostles.

The bishop guides and governs his diocese. He proclaims the word of God, personally and through his commissioned priests and deacons. But the bishop also shares concern for the larger, universal Church together with his fellow bishops. This bond of world-wide bishops united with the Pope is known as "Collegiality."

50. What is a Priest?

A Priest is one who has received the Sacrament of Holy Orders through which he has become an anointed administrator of the Sacraments and of the Church's blessings.

The terms "secular" and "regular" describe the two general kinds of Catholic clergy. Secular or diocesan priests live in and belong to a diocese and exercise their priestly functions under the jurisdiction of their bishop. Regular priests belong to a religious order or congregation such as Jesuits, Benedictines, Dominicans who normally live in religious houses. They follow an approved rule of life and works. All Catholic priests in the Latin rite take a vow of chastity, together with vows or promises of poverty and obedience.

A deacon is one who has received part of the Sacrament of Holy Orders not to become a full priest but, rather, for some ministry of service to God's people through the liturgy, word, and charity.

**Distinctive Marks of
Christ's Church**

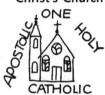

51. What are the four distinctive Marks of the Catholic Church?

The true Church of Christ has these four marks: it is one, holy, Catholic, and apostolic. And the only Church with these four marks is the Roman Catholic Church.

These four marks became part of the Nicene Creed as early as the year 381, when the First Council of Constantinople added the words, *"I believe in one, holy, Catholic, and apostolic Church. . . ."*

**Powers Given by Christ to
His Church**

52. What three main powers did Christ leave for His Church?

Christ assigned to His Church the threefold office of prophet, priest, and king

a) to teach what He taught (prophet),

b) to sanctify by His means, as by the Sacraments (priest),

c) and to govern the faithful, like a shepherd (King).

53. When is the Pope infallible?

The Pope is infallible in his pronouncements when, in his capacity as supreme shepherd and teacher of the entire Church, he declares or defines that a given doctrine concerning faith or morals must be held as true by all the faithful throughout the world.

The Church is preserved by the Holy Spirit from all grave error in its teachings on faith and morals.

The Church makes its infallible pronouncements either through the Pope and bishops together, or through the Pope alone.

The necessity of the grace of infallibility for Peter's role, and that of his successors, as supreme head and shepherd is self-evident. Without inerrancy in matters of faith and morals Peter and his successors can not rightly function as Rock and Foundation of Christ's Church, nor could Peter have strengthened his fellow Apostles in their faith, as Jesus had asked him to do.

Moreover, infallibility is joined to the office of Pope, not to the person. Peter would die, but the Church would endure until the end of the world. Together with the enduring Church of Christ, its head, rock and foundation, the Pope must be given the grace of perduring in infallibility.

People Who Are Saved

54. *Why is the Catholic Church known as "the Church of Salvation"?*

The Roman Catholic Church is called the Church of Salvation because she first received from Christ the mission and the means to bring people to eternal salvation.

Jesus Christ died for all and wants all to be saved. Those who never learned of God or the Church can be saved if they do God's will as made known to them through the natural moral law, following their conscience.

(For useful questions on the above chapter, see p. 144.)

Mary helps us gain real peace on earth and everlasting joy in eternity while fulfilling our Catholic lives now with Christ.

X.
OUR BLESSED MOTHER AND THE SAINTS

The Prerogatives of Mary, Mother of Jesus

55. Who was the only human person preserved from Original Sin?

The only solely human person who was preserved from Original Sin was Mary, the Mother of Jesus.

Concerning Mary's Immaculate Conception, Pope Paul VI stated in his published Creed of 1968, "We believe that Mary, who remained ever a Virgin, is the Mother of the Incarnate Word, our God and Savior, Jesus Christ, and by reason of this singular election she was, in consideration of the merits of her divine Son, redeemed in a more eminent manner, she was preserved from all stain of original sin and was filled with the gift of God's grace more than all other creatures." And since she was conceived without the stain of original sin, she never committed any personal sins.

The Immaculate Conception is the patronal feast day of the United States and is a holyday of obligation for American Catholics.

Our Devotion to Our Blessed Lady

56. Why is the Blessed Mother truly the Mother of God?

Since Jesus is God as well as man, His blessed Mother, Mary, is truly called the Mother of God.

Also, in addition, in order to help us on earth, Jesus gave us His own Blessed Mother when, dying on the Cross, He said, "Woman, behold, your son," "behold, your mother" (Jn 19:25-27).

The archangel Gabriel announced to Mary that she had been chosen to become the mother of God's Son.

"Then the angel said to her, 'Do not be afraid, Mary, for you have found favor with God. Behold, you will conceive in your womb and bear a Son, and you will name Him Jesus. . . .' Mary said to the angel, 'How will this be, since I am a virgin?' The angel answered, 'The Holy Spirit will come upon you, and the power of the Most High will overshadow you. Therefore, the Child to be born will be holy, and He will be called the Son of God . . . for nothing will be impossible for God.' Then Mary said, 'I am the servant of the Lord. Let it be done to me according to your word' " (Lk 1:30-38).

57. *What are some points about the Blessed Virgin Mary which Pope Paul VI touched on in his Apostolic Exhortation of February 2, 1974?*

On February 2, 1974, Pope Paul VI issued an Apostolic Exhortation in which he spoke of authentic veneration of Mary. Such veneration, he said is truly Christian, and he pointed to its place in the liturgy. Many forms of devotion should be rescued from neglect. Especially, the Pope called for greater use of the rosary and the Litany of the Blessed Virgin. Also, many Catholics wear a medal of our Blessed Lady and even touch it in time of need, asking her protection and assistance.

The Pope further urged devotion to Mary upon pastors and others engaged in pastoral work for the blessings it can bring. All in all, he affirmed what has always been the mind of the Church, that abuses aside, veneration of Mary points to Christ and redounds to His glory.

St. Joseph, Foster Father of Jesus and husband of Mary

58. *Who was the foster father of Jesus and husband of Mary?*

The foster father of Jesus was St. Joseph, husband to Mary.

The Saints, Our Heavenly Helpers

59. Who belong to the Communion of Saints?

To the Communion of Saints belong

a) the people on earth who believe in Christ (The Church Militant),

b) the souls in purgatory (The Church Suffering),

c) and the Saints in heaven (The Church Victorious).

Belief in the Communion of Saints goes far back to the very beginnings of the Church. The "Saints" in question are not only the canonized ones. The Bible generally uses the word for all who are united with God through sanctifying grace and belong to the people of God. This is the sense of "The Communion of Saints."

60. How does the worship of God differ from the veneration of Saints?

Catholics do not give to Saints the same honor which we give to God. We honor God with the worship of Him as the supreme Lord. We honor the Saints with much less veneration of them as God's faithful servants.

Jesus did not have an earthly father, such as we have. His father is God the Father in heaven. Sacred Scripture tells us very little about St. Joseph himself. It merely states that he was an upright or "just" man (Mt 1:19). In biblical language this means that he rendered to God and to fellow humans what was rightly theirs. This means showing justice and kindness to others, thereby leading them to obedience and love and worship of God. St. Joseph is also rightly known as Patron of the Universal Church. As well as praying to Mary we would do well to ask help from St. Joseph, worker and foster father on earth of Jesus.

When the Bible speaks of "brothers" of Jesus, this does not mean that Joseph and Mary had other children aside from Jesus. Though married, Joseph and Mary lived a virginal life together. In the Bible, "brothers" and "sisters" often mean no more than close relatives. Lot, for example is called brother of Abraham, though he was only a nephew (Gen 13:8).

Even God Himself honors and glorifies the Saints. Christ said, *"Whoever serves Me will be honored by My Father" (Jn 12:26)*. Veneration of the Saints also creates incentives to try to follow the example of their holy life. *"Can't you do what they did?"* St. Augustine used to urge, saying in effect that the Saints are not a breed apart but rather are weak human beings like the rest of us, but who tried and became strong and holy through cooperating with the same graces from God which are available to Catholics in these days of ours.

At the canonization ceremony of a Saint the Pope proclaims that the person lived a holy life of charity while on earth and is now with God in the glory of heaven's blessedness awaiting our own arrival there.

THE STATIONS OF THE CROSS

Much of God's grace comes to us from saying the Stations of the Cross which are:

1. Jesus Is Condemned to Death.
2. Jesus Takes Up His Cross.
3. Jesus Falls the First Time.
4. Jesus Meets His Blessed Mother.
5. Simon of Cyrene Helps Jesus Carry the Cross.
6. Veronica Wipes the Face of Jesus.
7. Jesus Falls for the Second Time.
8. Jesus Comforts the Women of Jerusalem.
9. Jesus Falls the Third Time.
10. Jesus Is Nailed to the Cross.
11. Jesus Is Stripped of His Garments.
12. Jesus Dies on the Cross.
13. Jesus Is Taken Down from the Cross.
14. Jesus Is Laid in the Tomb.

After a brief meditation on each station, an Our Father, Hail Mary, and a Glory Be to the Father should be said.

61. How can we help the Souls in Purgatory?

We can help the souls in purgatory by prayer, good works, and particularly by offering the holy sacrifice of the Mass for their speedy entrance into heaven's bliss.

62. Why does Purgatory seem logically proper?

And purgatory, as a good opportunity to clean up a bit before we enter God's heaven, seems logically proper. After all, who of us would want to go from the dust of this earth without preparing a little before entering the very presence of the Lord God!

(For questions on the above chapter, see p. 144.)

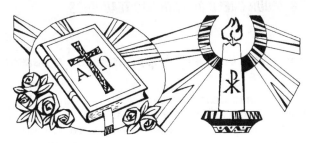

The word of God and the light of His Church can unite us eternally with Him and loved ones in heaven.

XI.
CHRIST'S RESURRECTION AND OURS IN THE HAPPINESS OF HEAVEN

Christ in Glory

63. When did Jesus Christ ascend into Heaven?

On the fortieth day after the Resurrection Jesus ascended unto His glory in heaven.

Christ's Ascension forty days after His Resurrection (Acts 1:3) was a visible departure, the end of His visible appearances to His Apostles.

64. What does it mean to say that Jesus sits at the right hand of His Father?

"And Jesus sits at the right hand of God, the Father almighty," means that, even as man, Jesus participates in the power and glory of the heavenly Father in heaven.

Our Death

65. What basically happens when a person dies?

In human death the soul departs from the body. We only know about our death that it is coming; we do not know when or where or how we will die.

Consequently, we should be ready at all times, as our Lord admonishes, *"Stay awake, for you know neither the day nor the hour" (Mt 25:13).*

66. What happens to our soul soon after we die?

After death our soul appears before the judgment seat of God.

This truth is clearly taught in the Bible. The Old Testament says in the Book of Sirach (11:26), *"On the day of death it is easy for the Lord to repay man according to his ways."* In the New Testament St. Paul writes, *"Each one of us will have to give an account of himself to God" (Rom 14:12).* And in Heb 9:27 we read, *"Human beings are destined to die but once, and after that to face subsequent judgment."* The primitive Greek text of this quotation from the Book of Hebrews makes it clear that "once" means "only once," that death is unrepeatable.

This rules out the notion of a reincarnation, an un-Christian belief according to which the soul after death re-enters another body, even a brute animal, as often as necessary until it has become completely cleansed.

Our Happiness in Heaven, Body Reunited with Soul

Those souls go straight to heaven who die in the state of sanctifying grace and are free of all sin and all punishment due to sin.

67. What will become of our body at the end of the world?

At the end of the world, on Judgment Day, our body will be raised up to share in the reward or punishment of our soul just as it shared in our good or evil deeds while on earth.

Just as in the beginning there was the wonder of creation, so at the end of the world there will be the wonder of the resurrection of the dead. We may, consequently, look forward to some bodily joys in heaven as well as here on earth.

Concerning heaven, Pope Paul VI said in his general audience of May 22, 1974, "*We now live in time but one day we shall live forever in the Kingdom of heaven. This does not mean the blue sky above but the new state of existence produced in a mysterious and wonderful manner according to God's creative plan and by His power. It is a Kingdom in which we share even now in virtue of certain supernatural conditions and gifts like faith, grace, and divine love. We are partly of earth and partly of heaven. We must know how to live simultaneously on earth and in heaven.*"

68. What are some joys of the blessed in heaven?

Considering some joys in eternity,

a) the blessed in heaven see God and live in indescribable joy;

b) and they are free of all evil while enjoying heaven's happiness together with loved ones.

"At the present time we see indistinctly, as in a mirror; then we shall see face to face" (1 Cor 13:12). *"Eye has not seen, ear has not heard, nor has the human heart imagined what God has prepared for those who love Him"* (1 Cor 2:9).

69. After mankind's resurrection, how will the bodies of the just people differ from the wicked?

Not all persons will be the same after our resurrection. The bodies of the just will be glorious and beautiful in heaven but the bodies of the wicked will be unsightly and abhorrent in hell.

The body that died was mortal; the body that is raised is immortal. The glorified body is both new and the same: new because it is glorified, the same because it is still the body we had, our body. And though the resurrected, immortal body is said to be "spiritual," it is not spiritual like an angel, in substance. In heaven, after the resurrection, human beings remain human beings, composites of soul and body, spirit and flesh, though flesh of which we have no experience except by an analogy with the resurrected body of Christ.

The Souls in Purgatory

70. Which souls go for a time to purgatory?

Those souls go to purgatory who die in the grace of God but are not free of all venial sin or all punishment due to sin. We may pray that soon they will be in heaven, where, one day, we also fully expect to join them, thanks to Christ Jesus.

What the Old Testament says in 2 Mac 12:46 presupposes after-death purification, as do the words of our Lord in Mt 12:13, because here also the possibility of satisfaction for sin in the hereafter is at least raised.

The Hell of the Damned

71. How can we know for sure that there is a hell of the damned?

That there is a hell we know from Sacred Scripture, and especially from the words of Jesus Himself.

Altogether, one can point to more than 70 places in the Bible that relate to hell. Christ Himself refers to hell 25 times as in Mt 10:28 wherein He cautions, *"Have no fear of those who kill the body but cannot kill the soul. Rather, fear the one who can destroy both soul and body in Gehenna."*

Certainly, the doctrine of an eternal hell is a deep mystery of faith, so great that only God can fathom it. An eternal hell is the ultimate outcome, a demand as it were, of His infinite holiness, expressing His utter hatred of sin. But only God fully comprehends this.

The General Judgment of
All Mankind

72. Why will there be a General Judgment for all mankind after the end of the world?

There will be a general judgment before Christ, the Lord

a) so that everyone will see that God is just, merciful, and wise;

b) and so that the good will receive deserved honor and the wicked deserved shame.

The General Judgment will take place at the end of time, whereas the Particular Judgment occurs immediately after death. In the General Judgment all who ever lived will appear before Christ. Our whole life, its good and bad, will pass in review.

The End of Our World

73. What do we know about the end of the world?

We know that the end of the world is coming, but we do not know when or how it will happen.

Belief in the end of our world is also found in ancient non-Christian religions. This could be a remnant of the original Revelation which God made to mankind.

(For useful questions on the above chapter, see p. 145.)

PART TWO
Our Code of Catholic Morality

WELCOME TO OUR HOME

A. CIVIL LAW (Abortion)
B. CHURCH LAW (FULL LIFE)
C. HELP THE NEEDY

PAX

*To live by our principles of Catholic Morality is to stay
clean from this world's fallacies.*

PART TWO

OUR CODE OF CATHOLIC MORALITY

SURELY the fulfilling of the duties of our state in life is high on the list of values within our Catholic code of morality.

Fundamentally, the ten Commandments of God and the Precepts of the Church are intended to direct the course of our moral life toward whatever is most suited for our true best interests during life. Caring mothers caution their beloved children not to do this or that, not to touch the hot stove or play with matches so they will not get burned. The good Lord and His guiding Church pleadingly warn us to do what is right and good for us but to avoid what is bad and harmful to us.

Increasing personal and communal honesty, justice, and charity as well as striving to acquire compassion for others and sexual purity along with other virtues all serve as buttressing pillars to uphold our faith, hope, and love throughout our lives.

Indeed, the moral virtues all are like strong stones along life's pathway to God's delightful heaven.

God's Commandments are all for our own good.

XII.

LOVE IN OUR LIVES AND GOD'S TEN COMMANDMENTS TO HELP US

An Informed Conscience, The Norm for Good Moral Living

74. What is a person's conscience?

Including the natural law, the highest norm by which we must conduct our lives is the law of God by following our conscience. Conscience is a judgment of human reasoning which declares the moral goodness or the moral evil of a human act.

75. What must we observe in following our conscience?

We must follow our conscience, but we also have a continuing obligation to conform our conscience to the moral law of God as expressed in the natural law within us and in Sacred Scripture as taught and applied by His Church.

Love in Our Lives

76. How do we show our love for God above everything else?

The greatest commandment is: " 'You shall love the Lord your God with all your heart, and with all your soul, and with all your mind.' This is the greatest and first commandment. The second is like it: 'You shall love your neighbor as yourself.' There is no other commandment greater than these" (Mt 22:37-39, Mk 12:30-31).

We show love for God above everything else when we value Him higher than anything in the world and are prepared to lose anything rather than to offend Him by serious sins.

77. How should we love ourselves correctly?

We love ourselves correctly when our first concern is for the holiness and salvation of our immortal soul, while living rightly.

While having due regard for our spiritual welfare, we must also be concerned with the body and things of this world such as health, possessions, studies, a good name, job security, etc. while showing some concern for our neighbor. But we should always remember our Lord's words, *"What will it profit a man if he gains the whole world and forfeits his very life?" (Mt 16:26).* And also, *"Those who commit sin and do evil deeds are their own worst enemies" (Tob 12:10).*

78. Who is our neighbor?

Our neighbor is everyone, friend or enemy.

In the parable of the Good Samaritan our Lord gives a graphic example of love of neighbor as He taught it (Lk 10:30-38). And in Mt 7:12, He announced for all time the Golden Rule, *"Treat others the way you would have them treat you."* From this it follows that whatever we do not want done to ourselves, we should not do to others.

79. Why should we love all people?

We should love all people

a) because God commands it,

b) because all people are children of the same God, are redeemed by the blood of the same Christ, and are called to the same eternal happiness,

c) and because by our good example we might win them to serve God and save their immortal souls.

"This is My commandment: love one another as I have loved you" (Jn 15:12). And also, *"Have we not all one Father? Did not one God create us? Why then do we break faith with one another . . . ?"* (Mal 2:10).

"Many pitiable persons may have lost faith in God because they have lost faith in the humanity of others; and many have found faith in God again because they came in contact with a good, truly human person" (Cardinal Faulhaber, d. 1952).

80. How can we show our love of neighbor?

We can show love of neighbor by practicing corporal and spiritual works of mercy, among other ways.

"My dear children, let us love not in word or speech but in deed and action" (1 Jn 3:18).

CORPORAL works of mercy are:

1. To feed the hungry.
2. To give drink to the thirsty.
3. To clothe the naked.
4. To visit the imprisoned.
5. To shelter the homeless
6. To visit the sick.
7. To bury the dead.

SPIRITUAL works of mercy are:

1. To admonish the sinner (by correcting those who need it when we can).

2. To instruct the ignorant (by teaching them where possible).

3. To counsel the doubtful (by advice to the needy when possible).

4. To comfort the sorrowful (by comforting the suffering we come across).

5. To bear wrongs patiently (by showing patience to all others).

6. To forgive all injuries (by forgiving others any hurt to yourself).

7. To pray for the living and the dead (by praying for others in need).

List of God's Helpful
Ten Commandments for
our Well-being

81. Which are the Ten Commandments of God?

The fundamentals of the Ten Commandments of God are:

1. I, the Lord, am your God. You shall not have other gods besides Me.

2. You shall not take the name of the Lord, your God, in vain.

3. Remember to keep holy the Sabbath day.

4. Honor your father and your mother.

5. You shall not kill.

6. You shall not commit adultery.

7. You shall not steal.

8. You shall not bear false witness against your neighbor.

9. You shall not covet your neighbor's wife.

10. You shall not covet your neighbor's goods.

Those who would disregard God's Commandments are their own worst enemy. Transgressions of God's Commandments harm not God the Lord but the transgressor. God asks for our love, and even pleads for it, not because He needs it but because by loving Him we find our happiness. This touches on the very heart of God's mystery, the love by which He first loves. Our lives would become easier if we did not look upon the Lord's Commandments as barriers to happiness but rather as helpful signposts to heaven.

God's Ten Commandments in Brief

**God Is First—
The 1st Commandment of
God for Our Good**

"I, the Lord, am your God. You shall not have other gods besides Me."

82. *What does the 1st Commandment require of people?*

The first Commandment requires that people believe in the one true God, hope in Him steadfastly, love Him above anything else, and worship Him alone.

Atheism's Loss

Atheism is the false philosophy which denies God's very existence.

The word derives from the Greek word "atheos," meaning no God or godless. The world can be considered as having atheists in theory and atheists in practice, those who actually live as though God did not matter.

Sins against Faith

83. When do people sin against faith?

People sin against faith

a) when they do not believe in God and His revealed truths (disbelief) or through their own fault lapse into false belief (heresy);

b) when they deny the faith or altogether renounce it (apostasy);

c) when they think that it does not matter what one believes or practices (religious indifferentism).

84. How can we preserve our faith?

To protect and preserve our faith we should pray regularly, take part in Church services, particularly the Holy Mass, try to read good spiritual books, and, certainly, attend classes on religious education faithfully when still obliged to do so.

What is the sin of sacrilege? The sin of sacrilege is the misuse or mistreatment of any person, place, or thing which is dedicated to the Lord or His worship.

What are some examples of committing a sacrilege? Some examples of committing a sacrilege would be: deliberately to receive Holy Communion in the state of mortal sin; physical assault on a person vowed to God; desecration of a Church, robbing from it, or committing a crime on the premises.

Honoring God's Holy Name —The 2nd Commandment of God for Our Good

"You shall not take the name of the Lord, your God, in vain."

85. When would a person sin against the 2nd Commandment?

Persons take the name of God in vain when they
a) deliberately speak it irreverently,
b) boldly utter blasphemy,
c) swear an oath falsely (perjury),
d) or fail to keep a serious vow made to God.

A person speaks the name of God irreverently when he or she uses it thoughtlessly or in anger, as a curse word. Although wrong, this may usually not be meant with disrespect to the Lord.

It can be a sin also to use sacred names with disrespect, such as the names of Jesus, Mary, or the Saints. Reverence, certainly, is due while speaking of the Scriptures, the Holy Eucharist, Christ's Cross, Holy Mass, etc.

We ought also to avoid crude or vulgar speech, particularly in the presence of children or in mixed company.

They would sin by blasphemy who by word or action would insult or show contempt for God or sacred persons, places, or things.

"Anyone who blasphemes the name of the Lord must be put to death. The entire community must stone him" (Lev 24:16). They also would be guilty of blasphemy who would deliberately scoff at the teachings or good practices of the Church. These can do much harm and should be discouraged from doing so in our presence.

By taking a vow is meant promising something good to God and binding ourselves to that promise under pain of sin. A vow is much more serious than a wish or intention and should only be taken after mature consideration and in consultation with one's confessor or spiritual director. Should the circumstances sufficiently change making the keeping of the vow impractical or overburdening, a release or commutation from that vow may be sought from a priest, possibly during a confession.

Some Sacredness on Weekends—The 3rd Commandment of God for Our Good

"Remember to keep holy the Sabbath day."

86. What does the 3rd Commandment require of Catholics?

The third Commandment requires that we Catholics keep holy the Lord's day by participating at Holy Mass on Sundays or their Saturday vigils, and on Holy Days.

"Sabbath" literally means rest. In the Old Testament the Lord's day was on Saturday in remembrance of the Lord's "rest" after His six days of creation, as given in the early chapters of Genesis. For followers of the New Testament, the Lord's day is on Sundays because Christ, our Lord, rose from the dead on a Sunday and also because the Holy Spirit was sent on the Apostles on Pentecost Sunday, the formal beginning of the Church.

(For more on Holy Mass and Holy Communion, see pp. 108ff.)

Sunday is kept holy by Catholics attending Holy Mass, performing good works, and gaining some relaxation.

Saturday afternoon or evening Mass substitutes as the vigil of Sunday worship. But the obligation still remains to keep Sundays holy in all other respects by physical and mental rest and recuperation of energies in peace. As much as possible, needless physical labor should be avoided on Sundays.

But, by not keeping Sunday or its vigil on Saturday as holy, we may deprive ourselves of God's blessing now and the loss of heaven hereafter.

(On the liturgical year, see p. 90.)

Obeying Parents and Those in Authority—The 4th Commandment of God for Our Good

"Honor your father and your mother."

87. What does the 4th Commandment require of people?

The fourth Commandment requires that we love, honor and, at a young age, obey our parents and lawful authorities.

The first three Commandments of God have referred to our correct relationship toward the Lord, God. The last seven Commandments will be concerned with our relationship toward our neighbor, as is also the second part of the Great Command of Christ.

88. What does the 4th Commandment require of children?

Children must love, respect, and obey their parents and those with lawful authority over them

a) because parents and lawful authorities speak in the name of God in regard to their children;

b) and because next to God parents and lawful superiors are the children's greatest benefactors, like priests and teachers.

Respecting Parents and Authorities

By God's design parents are the chief cooperators with Him in the upbringing of the children whom God has entrusted to their care. In that capacity, therefore, parents are the representatives of the Lord in regard to their children. Teachers also have delegated authority over their students from the parents by the mere enrollment of the children at their school.

89. What should children show their parents and rightful authorities?

Children should show their parents and those with authority over them their love, respect, and obedience

a) by obeying them gladly and promptly,

b) by striving to be a credit and a joy to them,

c) and by cooperating with them, praying for them, and assisting them in need.

90. How can children sin against their parents and elders?

Children can sin against their parents or elders when they

a) do not obey them or only poorly,

b) are ungrateful, rude, or stubborn toward them and cause sadness to them,

c) regard them with contempt, disdain, or wish evil to them,

d) or do not pray for them and try to help them, or neglect them in time of need.

It is to a young person's own benefit to respect parents, teachers, and other elders because God asks this and also because we can only learn from our elders when we have respect for them.

Just as children can be a great pride and joy to their parents, they can sometimes be the source of intense grief, sorrow, and agony. Also, many a mother or father has been brought to a premature grave by the ingratitude or ill-treatment on the part of some children who will surely regret their mistreatment of their parents when it is too late, just as those who were good to their parents will be glad about it the rest of their lives.

Besides parents, we owe respect and love to lawful superiors, namely teachers, parish priests, employers, and to those who have especially helped us.

"Let everyone submit himself to the governing authorities, for all authority derives from God, and whatever authorities exist have been instituted by God"(Rom 13:1).

Parents toward Children

91. What is the basic duty of parents toward their children?

The basic duty of parents toward their children is to love and provide for the spiritual and temporal well-being of their children.

Not only in parental supervision, but any persons with authority over others should have regard for the spiritual and the material welfare of those within their charge insofar as this is proper to their position.

Avoiding Harm to People—
The 5th Commandment of
God for Our Good

"You shall not kill."

92. What does the 5th Commandment forbid of us?

The fifth commandment forbids us to harm the body or soul of others or our own.

93. When is a sin committed against the physical or spiritual harm to others?

A sin is committed against physical harm to the body or spiritual harm to the soul of others

a) when someone assaults others physically, wounding or killing them;

b) or when someone abuses, frightens, or hurts them emotionally or leads others into sin; then the abuser of others must try to repair any harm done to them.

The killing of a human being may possibly become allowable in legitimate self-defense, or when absolutely necessary, or in defense of one's country when, however, the death of another is not directly intended.

94. Besides evil deeds, what else does the 5th Commandment forbid of us?

Furthermore, the fifth commandment forbids not only evil deeds but also malicious thoughts, impurities, bad desires, and actions which could lead to evil deeds, such as hatred, anger, desire for revenge, and quarreling, abusive language, sexual impurity, and wishing harm to another.

Harm to Ourselves

95. How can we sin against the respect due to ourselves?

We can sin against the respect which is due to ourselves if we should

a) seriously harm or shorten our life through excesses of any kind such as violent outbursts of anger, sexual impurity, or any other addiction to the appetites of our flesh,

b) needlessly endanger or harm our life, health, or good name, or that of our family,

c) or attempt to take or to harm our own life through means of self-destruction or serious danger to our health.

Proverbs 14:30 and Sirach 6:2 and 4 point out that fleshly appetites, like sexual impurity or habitual heavy drug-taking, can turn on us like killer-snakes. At first they entrap their victim, then they paralyze it, and finally they devour it whole and entire.

Harm against Others

96. How can we sin against the respect due to others?

The fifth commandment forbids harming not only the body of others but also their souls by carelessly giving scandal—such as when by word, deed or omission we become an occasion of sin for others. Certainly it would be sinful to lead others into a sinful situation, particularly the young, innocent, or uninitiated in the ways of evil.

About the scandal of bad example, Jesus said, *"If anyone causes one of these little ones who believe in Me to sin, it would be better for him to have a great millstone fastened around his neck and to be drowned in the depths of the sea. Woe to the world because of scandals. . . . Woe to that man through whom they come"* (Mt 18:6-7).

By giving scandal people help the devil to destroy souls for whom Christ died. The scandal-giver also shares in the sins which grow out of the scandal.

"He (the devil) was a murderer from the beginning . . . He is a liar and the father of lies" (Jn 8:44).

Do not become a soul-destroyer by giving bad example and keep away from those who do this harm.

"You have heard that your ancestors were warned: 'You shall not kill, and anyone who does so will be subject to judgment.' But I say this to you: Anyone who is angry with his brother will be subject to judgment" (Mt 5:21-22). And also, *"Anyone who hates his brother is a murderer, and you know that no murderer has eternal life abiding in him"* (1 Jn 3:15).

97. What must a person do after he or she has harmed the soul or body of someone else?

When a person has harmed the soul or body of someone else, such a person must repair that harm as far as possible, not only go to confession.

"This is how everyone will know that you are My disciples: your love for one another" (Jn 13:35).

Of course considerations of violence, terrorism, fighting, threatening, kidnapping, blackmailing, drug abuse, excessive drug-taking or adverse use of alcohol, gangsterism, abortion, torturing, and warring contain big sins against people and require that amends be made as soon as possible according to the harm done to others.

Sexual Self-control— The 6th and 9th Commandments of God for Our Good

Respecting the Human body

"You shall not commit adultery."
"You shall not covet your neighbor's wife."

98. Who are required to be sexually pure by the 6th and 9th Commandments?

In the sixth and ninth commandments God forbids sexual impurity, immodesty, and anything which can lead to such sins.

Basically, all people are called to be pure according to their state in life and loving intercourse is encouraged between those who are validly married.

But the unmarried are not allowed to take to themselves those rights which are reserved only for the married.

God requires all unmarried people to be sexually pure in thought, desire, and touch; also in what is read, seen in movies or on TV and in all conduct, thereby showing respect for our own or someone else's body with its proper dignity.

Aids for Sexual Purity

99. What should we do in order to keep ourselves sexually pure?

In order to help keep ourselves pure and chaste, we should avoid near occasions of sin, pray fervently, be devoted to the Blessed Virgin Mary, go to confession frequently, and receive holy communion as often as possible. Weekly Holy Communion is strongly advocated.

100. What should persons think about when sexually tempted?

When tempted against purity, people should change their thoughts to something more wholesome, calmly think of Jesus and other holy or pleasant things. Thoughts of death and eternal judgment have helped some tempted people, while thinking of sports or songs have helped others.

It is well known that threats to chastity can come from harboring bad thoughts, from conversations, and touches as well as from bad magazines, pictures, movies, TV or anything which can harm decent thinking.

A sincere prayer, said slowly and calmly may help along the lines of the following: *"O Mary, my Mother, I come to you for help. I dedicate my eyes, ears, heart, hands, and my entire self to your divine Son's Sacred Heart. Please direct my thoughts toward some good reading, or taking a walk, or phoning a friend. And thank you, dear blessed mother, for your help in conquering this temptation. Amen."*

It would also be well to pray from time to time to Saints who fought valiantly when tempted, like St. Aloysius Gonzaga, St. Stanislaus Kostka, St. Maria Goretti or Blessed Kateri Tekakwitha, the American Indian maiden.

**Respecting Others' Property—
The 7th and 10th Commandments
of God for Our Good**

"You shall not steal."

"You shall not covet your neighbor's goods."

101. What do the 7th and 10th Commandments forbid?

The seventh and tenth commandments forbid harming or desiring to harm others in regard to their goods and property.

"Goods and property" make up everything which a person owns: home and land, clothing, athletic equipment, tools, etc. God gives humans the right to personal ownership and others may not violate this right. The owner, however, should also be considerate of those less well off. *"Your almsgiving should be in proportion to your means. If you have been blessed with great abundance, give much; if you possess little, do not be afraid to give even some of that"* (Tob 4:8).

Avoiding Harm to Others

102. When would we harm others in regard to their belongings?

We harm others in regard to their belongings if

a) we rob or steal,

b) defraud or profiteer unfairly,

c) fail to return found or borrowed belongings,

d) neglect to pay our debts, such as borrowed money,

e) or deliberately damage the property or belongings of another.

Cooperating in the Sin of Another

103. How would people sin by cooperating in the sin of theft by another?

They also would sin who

a) advise, approve, or assist in doing harm to others,

b) knowingly receive, buy, or deal in goods which have been stolen,

c) or do not prevent the harm though they could and should.

104. What must we do if we have harmed others in regard to their possessions?

If we have harmed others in regard to their belongings, money, or property, we must make restitution by restoring them as soon as possible.

Any unjustly acquired goods or money must be returned to the owner. If that is impossible, we must then give them over to the poor or to other good works. We ourselves may not keep any ill-gotten money or goods. When restitution is involved, it must be made without delay; if full return is not now possible, then the offended party should be contacted and some acceptable payments agreed upon.

Actual theft or default usually begins within the heart and slyness is a sure sign of intended harm-doing.

Good Speech—The 8th Commandment of God for Our Good

"You shall not bear false witness against your neighbor."

105. What does the eighth Commandment about lying forbid?

The eighth Commandment forbids

a) lying or false witness,

b) and any sin against the character, person, or good name of another.

A lie is saying or pretending against another what one knows to be untrue in order to deceive harmfully.

A serious direct lie is always wrong, even if perpetrated under the pretext of preventing a greater evil or a supposed good.

However, not everything that is not literally true is necessarily a lie. Tall amusing tales do not deceive anyone, hence are not real lies. Even certain conventional greetings, compliments, excuses, and the like are not taken seriously. In some circumstances, as to keep a secret or to maintain necessary privacy, a mild form of evasive speech may be used. Everyone realizes or should that to say, "Mr. Jones is not here just now," really means that he is not now available to see or speak to the caller.

Certainly, people should guard against harmful, deceitful, deep lying since this fosters the devil's work, is forbidden, and weakens character.

As for gossip, it can be very damaging and we are easily led to participate in it, for example, by lending a too-willing ear, asking encouraging questions, adding something to it all, and doing other sly things. Gossip can cause seemingly endless ill-feelings, and certainly any harm that has been caused needs to be corrected as soon as possible before it spreads like wildfire.

Do unto Others As You Would Have Them Do unto You

106. How can we sin against the person, name, or character of others?

We can sin against the person, name, or character of others

a) by false accusations, suspicion, and rash judgments,

b) and by slander and malicious gossip, or tale telling about others.

"Do not judge, so that you in turn may not be judged. For you will be judged in the same way that you judge others" (Mt 7:1-2).

"I tell you that on the day of judgment people will have to render an account for every careless word they utter" (Mt 12:36).

People can sin through false suspicion when without solidly good reasons, they presume evil about others or through wrongful rash judgments they deem a merely supposed evil from hearsay gossip to be certain against another.

Slander is to assert or encourage something bad about others which is either not true at all or to exaggerate some evil which may be true.

"The tongue is a small member but its pretensions are great. . . . It is a restless evil, full of deadly poison" (Jas 3:5, 8). And also, *"Why do you take note of the splinter in your brother's eye but do not notice the wooden plank in your own eye?"* (Mt 7:3).

(For useful questions on the above chapter, see, p. 145.)

Seeking discernment from God's Church brings deliverance from confusion, making life more fruitful.

XIII.
PRECEPTS OR GUIDING LAWS OF THE CATHOLIC CHURCH TO ASSIST US

The Purpose and List of Church Precepts for Catholics in the United States

107. Why should Catholics obey Church laws or Precepts?

We should obey Church laws or precepts as guiding gifts from the Lord

a) because the Church's laws and powers come ultimately from Jesus,

b) and because the common good and unity of the Church require that her important activities be regulated by laws which are imposed on us out of love.

Guiding rulers of the Church and their appointed representatives have a right to our obedience of Church laws because, firstly, their binding power to command observance derives directly or indirectly from Jesus, and secondly because the common welfare of the Church community requires that the spiritual activity of the Church be regulated by law even in matters which may seem of minor importance. The justice of law precludes arbitrariness and so ensures the necessary uniformity of treatment of everyone in the same manner.

108. What are the present Precepts of the Church in the United States?

The current precepts of the Church in the United States are:

1. To participate at Mass on all Sundays or their Saturday vigils and on holydays of obligation.

2. To confess our sins at least once a year, and to receive Holy Communion frequently but at least during the Easter Season.

3. To study Catholic teaching before and after Confirmation.

4. To observe all laws of the Church concerning Marriage.

5. To contribute to the support of the Church with interest and money.

6. To fast and to abstain on the days appointed.

7. To join in the missionary spirit and apostolate of the Church and wherever possible according to each one's circumstances.

Participating at Mass— The 1st Precept of the Church to Assist Us

"To keep holy the day of the Lord's Resurrection: to worship God by participating in Mass every Sunday and Holy Day of Obligation; to avoid those activities that would hinder renewal of soul and

body on the Sabbath (that is needless work and business activities, unnecessary shopping, etc.)."

109. What does the 1st Precept of the Church about Mass require of Catholics?

The first precept of the Church requires that we be not only physically present at Mass but also present in mind and heart by sincere participation in the celebration of the Holy Eucharist on weekends and required Holy Days.

If our employment requires us to work on weekends, we may not thereby hold ourselves excused from that part of the precept which requires us to participate in Holy Mass if we can do so without grave inconvenience. Nowadays employers generally are receptive to requests for time off to attend sacred worship. Besides, the Saturday afternoon or evening availability of that vigil of Sunday can solve this problem for many.

And also, Sunday should not be considered merely as a gloomy day of obligation but rather as a day of joy in celebrating the Lord's Resurrection.

Catholic Holy Days in the
United States

110. Which are the Holy Days in the United States?

In addition to participating at Mass every weekend, Catholics in the United States are obliged to attend the Holy Sacrifice on the following Holy Days:

Solemnity of Mary, Mother of God . . . . .Jan. 1
Ascension Thursday . . . . .40 days after Easter
Assumption of Mary into heaven . . . .Aug. 15
All Saints Day .Nov. 1
Immaculate Conception of Mary . . . . .Dec. 8
Nativity of Jesus (Christmas) . . . . . . .Dec. 25

Holy Days are special feasts celebrated by Catholics. Formerly there were many more, but the circumstances of the industrial ages led to a curtailment of that number by Church authorities.

Bound by serious obligation to participation at Mass on Sundays or their Saturday vigils and the Holy Days are all Catholics who have reached the age of reason and are not otherwise excused.

Are Catholics still obliged to go to Mass on Sunday or its Saturday vigil? Yes, indeed. This is so because the very nature of being a Catholic is to belong to the Eucharistic Church-community whose heart and center is that celebration of the Holy Eucharist together. It is in this sense that our weekend Mass-offering should be considered as a holy obligation.

Although the Holy Eucharist is a precious love-feast, the Lord understands that sometimes we simply cannot be present, much as we certainly would like to be. Our attendance at Mass is not by some cruel law with punishment hanging over us for any infringement, however involuntary. Practicing Catholics realize the importance of our Mass. And they will know when there may be a legitimate and reluctant excusing cause preventing attendance at Mass.

Our Church Liturgical Year

111. Of what is the Catholic Liturgical Year comprised?

The Catholic Liturgical Year is comprised of the succession of seasons and feasts celebrated annually from one advent to another.

Each year through the liturgy, especially of the Mass, the Church makes present for us the precious Life, Messages, Death, and glorious Resurrection of our Lord Jesus Christ wherein we celebrate the sacred mysteries and obtain graces for ourselves, loved ones, and the whole world.

Outline of the Church Liturgical Year

Advent—Jesus is near.

Christmas—Jesus is with us.

Epiphany—Jesus shows Himself forth to the world.

Ordinary Time—Jesus gives lessons for His Church.

Lent—Jesus suffers and dies to save us.

Easter—Jesus rises unto His Resurrection, triumphing over peoples' sins and death.

Easter Season—Jesus instructs His Apostles for our well-being.

Ascension—Jesus ascends to His heavenly Father.

Pentecost—Jesus sends the Holy Spirit on His early Church.

Ordinary Time—The Spirit carries on the work of Jesus through His Church.

Confession and Holy Communion—The 2nd Precept of the Church to Assist Us

"To lead a Sacramental life: to receive Holy Communion frequently and the Sacrament of Reconciliation or Penance regularly; minimally, to receive the Sacrament of Reconciliation at least once a year (annual confession is obligatory only if serious sin is involved [though we are urged to confess every few months or oftener]); minimally also to receive Holy Communion at least once a year, [known as 'making our Easter duty'] between the first Sunday of Lent and Trinity Sunday [but we are urged to receive Holy Communion about every week].

112. What does the 2nd Precept of the Church about Confession and Holy Communion require of us?

The Second Precept of the Church requires that we lead a sacramental life, that is, that we encounter Jesus frequently through the Sacraments and especially that Catholics

a) receive the Sacrament of Reconciliation (go to confession) at least once a year (only if a serious sin is involved),

b) and receive Holy Communion at least once a year during the period loosely prescribed as Easter time.

"At least" is used above in the minimal sense but the Church strongly recommends more frequent sacramental confession and, certainly, weekly or even daily receiving of Holy Communion. There may be legitimate excusing reasons for not having to attend Mass on occasion.

(For more on Confession, Mass, and Holy Communion, see pp. 112, 116, 118.)

Frequent going to confession is a great spiritual help. It makes us more responsive to God's voice and grace thereby helping us not only to preserve our Catholic Faith but also to live this faith more completely, joyfully, and peacefully.

113. What are some conditions for receiving Holy Communion worthily?

Some conditions for receiving Holy Communion worthily are:

a) being in the state of grace,

b) having a devotional intention,

c) and observing the eucharistic fast.

STATE OF GRACE: being here and now free from mortal sin. But our Communions will bring us more grace and blessings, and our spiritual growth will become greater, if we also strive to overcome any deliberate venial sins in our life.

DEVOTIONAL INTENTIONS: not out of mere habit or distracting human respect, but to please our Lord, to live a more full Catholic life, to help others and, indeed, to assist the entire world-wide Church to grow.

EUCHARISTIC FAST: abstaining from food and drink, except water and needed medicine, for one hour before Holy Communion. Plain water never breaks the communicant's fast.

**Religious Education—
The 3rd Precept of the Church
to assist us**

"To study Catholic teaching in preparation for the Sacrament of Confirmation, to be confirmed, and then to continue to study and advance the cause of Christ."

114. What does the 3rd Precept of the Church about Religious Education require?

The third Precept requires that Catholics

a) study the faith both before and after their confirmation

b) and advance the cause of Christ, the Church, throughout their lives.

The Church gives us a faith with understanding which, in turn, seeks to be put into practice thereby advancing Christ's Church.

We grow, assuredly, in love of Christ and His Church the more we pray and have learned of them both by advancing through knowing our faith as found in most modern catechisms. Catholics seek to learn about not just a theory or Philosophy but a Person, Jesus Christ Himself. To believe is to come to Jesus and to listen to Him Who speaks "the words of God" (Jn 3:34). *To believe is to look at and experience Jesus Who "sees the Father."*

Marriage Rules—The 4th Precept of the Church to Assist Us

"To observe the marriage laws of the Church; to give religious training, by word and example, to one's children and to use parish schools and catechetical programs."

115. What does the 4th Precept of the Church about Marriage Rules require of those couples who wish to receive the Sacrament of Matrimony?

The Fourth Precept of the Church requires that Catholics who receive the Sacrament of Matrimony should

a) abide by the Church's teachings on marriage and comply with her requests for getting married properly,

b) provide religious training and good example for their children at home,

c) and see that their children receive a formal Catholic education.

The Church, in virtue of the commission received from Christ, teaches the wishes of God and is empowered to lay down certain conditions for the sacramental marriage of her Catholics.

Several things can stand in the way of a successful marriage, the most obvious of which would be a valid previous marriage of either partner. For more particulars, especially before planning a marriage, Catholics should always consult with their parish priest in plenty of time, even 6 months, if possible, before their happy day.

(For more on the Sacrament of Matrimony, see pp. 131 to 136.)

Supporting the Church— The 5th Precept of the Church to Assist Us

"To strengthen and support the Church—one's own parish community and parish priests, the worldwide Church, and the Pope."

116. What does the 5th Precept about supporting the Church require of us?

The fifth Precept of the Church requires that each one of us help to meet both the financial and the spiritual needs of the Church.

Most parishes use envelopes for gathering the monetary contributions of parishioners for support of vital parish programs. However, "Church support" should also include the needed lending of a parishioner's time and talents as of a doctor, lawyer, plumber, mechanic, or for whatever the priests may need. And also, the youth of the parish usually have many strong talents for helping their parish programs and assisting their own priests who really become delighted when generously assisted by their youthful parishioners.

Doing Penance—The 6th Precept of the Church to Assist Us

"To do penance, including abstaining from meat, and fasting from food on the appointed days."

117. What does the 6th Precept of the Church about doing penance ask of us?

The sixth Precept of the Church asks that Catholics sometimes practice the virtue of penitence, which means combining

a) the inner conversion of the spirit

b) with the voluntary exercise of external acts of self-denial, such as to fast and abstain on the days appointed for the Church community.

Fasting and other penitential practices are good ways to remind ourselves and others that God has called us all to supernatural living in the midst of a secularistic, sexistic, and consumeristic atmosphere.

However, it is mostly left to each Catholic's own choice just precisely which acts of mortification, moderation, or self-denial to practice. Certainly performing acts of charity such as visiting the sick or those in institutions, teaching religious studies to a group of lively teenagers, etc. will surely qualify as worthwhile penitential and apostolic activities.

118. Regarding fasting, what is required of Catholics from ages 21 to 59?

On those days requiring Catholics from age 21 to 59 to fast, they should limit themselves to one full meal a day.

In addition to one full meal, two lighter meals are also allowed. But snacking between meals breaks the fast required. Including pregnant women, any sick person is excused from fasting until recovered. Even those bound to fast may have sufficient grounds for being excused such that fasting might impair their regular working hours or their health. In doubt, a priest or other experienced adult Catholic may be consulted.

In the United States, the days of fasting prescribed by authorities are Ash Wednesday and Good Friday.

119. From ages 14 and upward, when should Catholics abstain from eating meat?

On appointed days of abstinence from age 14 onward. Catholics should not eat meat on Ash Wednesday, Good Friday, and all other Fridays in Lent.

Nevertheless, conditions of health, unavailability of decent food other than meat, etc., may excuse a person.

Cooperating in Apostolic Works— The 7th Precept of the Church to Assist Us

"To join in the missionary spirit and the apostolate of the Church."

120. What does the 7th Precept of the Church's Apostolate request of all Catholics?

The Seventh Precept of the Church asks that

a) all Catholics take part in the Church's missionary spirit and its various apostolates,

b) through prayer, the witness of a good Catholic life, and active practice of evangelization, thereby spreading the Catholic faith.

The faithful of the Church should engage in spreading Christ's Church because we are commanded by our Lord to do so, both formerly and more recently again by the great Vatican Council II.

(For useful questions on the above chapters, see p. 146.)

PART THREE
Our Cult of Catholic Worship

To grow in the spirit of Catholic Worship is to advance in the ability to love truly.

PART THREE

OUR CULT OF CATHOLIC WORSHIP

SINCE the beginning of time, human beings have given worship to their deity. Our inward and outward acts of dependence on God are principally found in our precious cult of worship such as our Holy Sacrifice of the Mass and receiving of Holy Communion, our going to confession, and all the other outstanding Sacraments along with prayer and the other liturgical aids.

Not all available devotions can be sufficiently stressed in an outline of Catholic worship.

But certainly our weekend and Holyday participation at Mass and Holy Communion is the Catholic's chief act of worshiping God. Our daily private prayers keep us attuned to our Lord just as the practice of meditating deepens this union. The assessment of our spiritual life, while confessing our sins at least every few months, will guide us toward the Lord's fountain of refreshing grace and strength and peace.

We also keep alive in Christ by receiving or attending the acceptance by others of the Sacraments such as a baptism, a confirmation, the anointing of the sick or aged, the funeral of a friend, an ordination of a young priest, or the wedding of a beautiful couple.

Other liturgical rites such as Benediction of the Blessed Sacrament, or the anniversary of a church, or the blessing of a child, youth, aged person, or automobile and so on are also beneficial grace-giving rites. They all portray the worship of our inner outpouring to our Lord by the various available means of Our Cult of Catholic Worship.

*Our Holy Mass and the seven Sacraments
are precious to us Catholics.*

XIV.
GOD'S GRACES FOR US FROM CHRIST'S SEVEN SACRAMENTS AND THE HOLY MASS

What a Sacrament is and Does For Us

121. What is the nature of any of the Sacraments?

A Sacrament is an outward special sign instituted by Jesus Christ to signify and to give inward grace.

A sign indicates something other than itself, as smoke indicates fire. The sacramental sign is a sense-perceptible material thing, though blessed for a holy usage, like water, bread and wine, oil, or spoken words, which point to and actually bring the graces of each particular Sacrament. Our Lord established the use of these outward signs for our receiving of useful grace. We should make good use of the Sacraments frequently and strive to learn all about each one.

122. Which are the seven Sacraments that Jesus Christ instituted for us?

Jesus Christ Himself instituted the seven Sacraments for us, which are:

1. Baptism
2. Confirmation
3. Holy Eucharist
4. Reconciliation or Penance
5. Anointing of the Sick or Aged
6. Holy Orders
7. Matrimony.

BAPTISM

The Sacrament of the Life-giving graces of Christ within Us

123. What does the Sacrament of Baptism do for us?

Baptism is the Sacrament in which we

a) are incorporated in Christ and made members of His Church,

b) are empowered to participate in Catholic worship,

c) and are born to eternal life by water and the Holy Spirit, thereby made heirs of heaven.

The person baptizing pours water over the head of the person being baptized and at the same time says, *"I baptize you in the name of the Father, and of the Son, and of the Holy Spirit."*

Baptism is known as the Sacrament of initiation or beginning in the Christian community, which is interested in the supernatural rebirth of the child and therefore in its timely Baptism.

124. Why is Baptism the most fundamental of the Sacraments?

Baptism is the most fundamental Sacrament because without Baptism no one can be saved.

"Go forth into every part of the world and proclaim the Gospel to all creation. Whoever believes and is baptized will be saved; whoever does not believe will be condemned" (Mk 16:15).

Concerning the fate of infants who die unbaptized, nothing has been revealed. However, many contemporary theologians hold that God's goodness makes it possible for these infants to be saved; just how we do not know. But we do know that God does want everyone to be saved and also that infants are not able to commit personal sin. Hence, the opinion is rightly put forward that all unbaptized infants will, by God's grace, be given the chance to accept Christ and thus be given the opportunity to be able to enter into heaven for eternity.

The abode of unbaptized infants is called Limbo. It was the place of rest where the souls of all the just remained until heaven was reopened after the death of Christ.

In addition to the usual Baptism by water, there are also Baptism of Blood and Baptism of Desire.

Baptism of Blood: From the beginning of Christianity, the community held that Baptism of Blood, which is martyrdom for Christ, makes up for the lack of Baptism by water. They could point to our Lord's words, *"Whoever loses his life for My sake will save it" (Lk 9:24)*. The Holy Innocents and the Catechumens who were martyred for Christ received this Baptism of Blood. The renowned historian Tertullian, speaking of martyrdom, says,

"This is the Baptism that takes the place of the actual Baptism that was not received" (chap. 16).

Baptism of Desire: This Baptism is received by persons who truly want to be baptized but are prevented, for example by an untimely death. If they have had a sincere desire for Baptism together with sorrow for sins committed, that desire is equivalently considered by God as actual Baptism by water. The desire exists most certainly when it is explicit or conscious, though it may only be implicit or unconscious, such as in persons who through no fault of their own have not known Christ or the Church, and yet strive by God's grace to do His will as best they have known it.

125. What are some effective fruits given to those who become baptized?

Some effective fruits of Baptism are:

a) Baptism imprints on the soul an indelible mark as a follower of Christ and a member of the Catholic Church community;

b) it takes away original sin, all personal sins, and any temporal or eternal punishment that may have been due to sins which have been repented;

c) and it confers ample grace in the baptized soul, particularly the infused virtues of supernatural faith, hope, and charity.

"You have been washed clean, you have been sanctified, you have been justified in the name of the Lord Jesus Christ and in the Spirit of our God" (1 Cor 6:11).

Baptism is the Sacrament of incorporation in Christ. It also makes us members of the Body of Christ, members of the Catholic Church. Christ is the head, we are the members. He is the vine, we are the branches.

Though Baptism remits all sin and any punishments due to repented sins, nevertheless, some side effects remain as consequences of our original sin, such as death, temptations to do evil, and the sufferings and tribulations of life as means of our gaining more merit.

126. What does the indelible mark imprinted on the soul through Baptism do?

The indelible mark or character imprinted on the soul through Baptism is like a seal which identifies the Christian as belonging to Christ our Lord, and as a member of the Catholic Church community.

The Book of Revelation speaks of that seal impressed *"on the foreheads of the servants of our God" (Rev 7:3).* The baptismal seal is not visible but the Christian's conduct is, and it should give testimony to the invisible seal which claims us permanently as belonging to Christ.

Godparents, together with the parents, should make the baptismal promises for the child and be helpful to the parents in the care and religious upbringing of the child.

CONFIRMATION

**The Sacrament of
Responsible Caring**

127. What does the Sacrament of Confirmation do for those confirmed?

Confirmation is the Sacrament by which the Catholic is strengthened for the mature profession and practice of the Catholic faith.

"To profess one's faith" means to bear witness to it in our life, so that people can see that we are practicing Catholics. Some obvious ways of doing this are: by going to Mass regularly every Sunday or Holyday, attending religious growth lectures, receiving the Sacraments regularly, defending the Catholic Church or the Pope, and in general by living well what our Catholic faith might require.

128. What are the effects of receiving the Sacrament of Confirmation?

The effects of receiving the Sacrament of Confirmation are:

a) that it produces an indelible mark or character on the soul which identifies the follower as a soldier of Jesus Christ Himself;

b) that it gives a fuller outpouring of the Holy Spirit to help the confirmed to remain faithful to the practice of the Catholic religion;

c) that it increases sanctifying grace within the confirmed;

d) and that it gives a more intimate potential for union with Christ Jesus in the Holy Eucharist.

From the time of the Apostles, in fulfillment of Christ's desire, Confirmation has imparted the gift of the Holy Spirit by the laying on of hands in order to complete the grace of the baptized.

129. How is Confirmation conferred?

Confirmation is conferred through the anointing by the Bishop with chrism or blessed oil on the forehead, which is done with the laying on of hands, together with the words, "be sealed with the gift of the Holy Spirit."

Thus signed with the holy oil, the baptized persons receive in Confirmation an indelible seal or character of the Lord, together with the gift of the Spirit which conforms them more closely to Christ giving them the grace to spread Christ's Church.

THE HOLY EUCHARIST

The Sacrament of Christ Himself Present to Us

130. What is the Holy Eucharist?

The Holy Eucharist is the Sacrament of the Body and Blood, Soul and Divinity of our Lord Jesus Christ truly present under the appearances of the consecrated bread and wine.

Jesus offers Himself on the altar as our sacrifice and to give Himself to us as our sacrificial food for strength in Holy Communion. The changing of bread and wine into Christ's Sacred Body and Blood is known as transubstantiation.

The Holy Eucharist is both a memorial and a here-and-now celebration of the Lord's Passion, Death, and glorious Resurrection. Through, with, in, and by the Church, Christ's redemptive sacrifice on the Cross becomes present again in every celebration of the Holy Mass,

Jesus promised to give us the Holy Eucharist in His words, *"The bread that I will give is My flesh, for the life of the world. Then the Jews started to argue among themselves, saying, 'How can this man give us His flesh to eat?' Jesus said to them, 'Amen, amen, I say to you, unless you eat the flesh of the Son of Man and drink His blood, you do not have life within you. Whoever eats My flesh and drinks My blood has eternal life, and I will raise him up on the last day. For My flesh is real food, and My blood is real drink' "* (Jn 6:51-55).

In its Constitution on the Sacred Liturgy, Vatican Council II says, *"At the Last Supper, on the night when He was betrayed, our Savior instituted the Eucharistic sacrifice of His body and blood. He did this in order to perpetuate the sacrifice of the Cross throughout the centuries until He should come again, and so to entrust to His beloved spouse, the Church, a memorial of His death and Resurrection: a Sacrament of love, a sign of unity, a bond of charity, a paschal banquet in which Christ is eaten, the mind is filled with grace, and a pledge of future glory is given to us"* (number 7).

**Jesus Himself Instituted
the Holy Eucharist**

131. When did Jesus institute the Holy Eucharist?

Jesus instituted the Holy Eucharist on the night before He died.

After Holy Thursday, the greatest commemoration of our Lord's Holy Eucharist is Easter Sunday, the day on which Jesus rose from death. The Solemnity of the Body and Blood of Christ also celebrates the institution of Holy Communion.

Christ instituted the Holy Eucharist at the Last Supper when Jesus took bread, blessed it, broke it, gave it to His disciples and said, *"Take this, all of you, and eat it; this is My body which will be given up for you."* In the same way Jesus took the cup, blessed it, gave it to His disciples and said, *"Take this, all of you, and drink from it; this is the cup of My blood of the new and everlasting covenant. It will be shed for you and for all so that sins may be forgiven. Do this in memory of Me"* (cf. Mt 26:26-38; Mk 14:22-24; Lk 22:19-20; 1 Cor 11:23-26).

132. When did Jesus change the bread and wine into His Sacred Body and Precious Blood?

When Jesus spoke the words, "This is My Body, this is My Blood," He changed the bread into His Sacred Body and the wine into His Precious Blood.

133. How do we know for certain that Jesus Christ is truly present in the Holy Eucharist?

That Jesus is truly present in the Holy Eucharist we know

a) from the words of Jesus both when He promised and when He actually instituted this great Sacrament

b) and from the clear teaching of the evangelists and the Apostle St. Paul and of the Church.

According to the clear words of Jesus, the Holy Eucharist is exactly the same Body and the same Blood with which Christ as Man was born, suffered, died, and rose from the dead.

134. What does the Church teach today about Christ's presence in the Holy Eucharist?

The Church today teaches what she has always taught from the time of the Apostles, namely that in the Holy Eucharist Jesus Christ is truly, actually, and uniquely present whole and entire.

"What seems bread is not bread, though it tastes so, but is the body of Christ; what seems wine is not wine, though it seems so to the taste, but is the blood of Christ" (St. Cyril of Jerusalem, d. 386). And also "Christ was holding Himself in His own hands as He held out His sacred Body and said, 'This is My Body'" (St. Augustine, d. 430).

Jesus chose bread and wine as the outward signs of this Sacrament because they best symbolize the inward grace of the Sacrament as our spiritual food for needed strength.

Just as the human soul is totally present in every part of the human body, so also is Jesus totally present in the least particle of the consecrated Host and in every drop of the consecrated Blood.

Our Holy Sacrifice of the Mass

135. What is the Sacrifice of the New Covenant?

The Sacrifice of the New Covenant is the Holy Sacrifice of Jesus Christ on the Cross, which becomes present on the altar as an unbloody sacrifice of the Mass, the Holy Eucharist.

Simply stated, the Mass is the same sacrifice as that of the Cross. The "Ite, missa est" or "Go in peace the Mass is ended" admits of the interpretation "Go, it is mission time," time for the people to go out into their world of daily life to fulfill their mission as Christians, other Christs.

When considering the links between the Last Supper, the Sacrifice of the Cross, and our Holy Mass we must remember that we are dealing with a profound mystery of faith and that it can never be explained to full satisfaction. There comes a point in which our limited abilities cannot go any further and only our faith in Christ's words can satisfy.

136. For how long have Catholics been offering the Holy Sacrifice of the Mass?

The people of the Catholic Faith have offered the Holy Sacrifice of the Mass ever since the time of the Apostles.

With our Lord's words, *"Do this in memory of Me" (Lk 22:19)*, Christ gave the Apostles and their bishops and priests as successors the power and the command to continue to offer the Holy Mass until time ends.

The Holy Sacrifice of the Mass is offered to God the Father.

At Mass we can also ask the Saints for their intercession, pray for our loved ones, for the forgiveness of mankind's sins, and for world peace or any other intention we may wish to remember.

What We Profit from the Benefit of Holy Mass

137. Who benefit from the spiritual fruits of the Mass?

All members of the Church, living and dead, benefit from the spiritual fruits of the Mass.

Those persons who devoutly participate at Mass or have Mass offered for someone's benefit also gain in a special way. It is a good practice to have Mass offered for some spiritual or temporal need as for a deceased loved one, for someone in need, or in thanksgiving to God.

138. How can Catholics best participate at Mass?

We can best celebrate the Mass by a full, active, and alert participation which is both external and internal as well as by receiving Holy Communion.

We should be united in faith and love together and try to avoid any appearance of division. It is as a group that the word of God is addressed to us and that we are invited to respond, to pray, to sing, to perform sacred actions, and to take certain positions. It is, moreover, precisely as a group of united Catholics that we should respond wholeheartedly.

139. Where especially do we encounter Christ in His saving mysteries?

It is in the Mass that we encounter Christ together in His saving mysteries and that we receive more strength, grace, and peace.

The more we can arouse our love for Christ and His Church, and the more wholeheartedly we can participate in the Mass, all the more are we likely to receive abundant blessings and graces from our dear Lord.

140. Why does the Mass also instruct us?

The Mass instructs us in points of the faith, because the Church hopes to teach even as she helps to sanctify us.

The Liturgy of the Word during Mass is a chief source of Catechetical instruction or teachings on the faith. The unfolding of the liturgical year instructs, uplifts, and forms Catholics by bringing them into relationship with the person of our Savior through the actualization of successive events in the life of Christ from His eagerly awaited birth at Christmas through His wonderful life as Mystical Head poured out at Pentecost through the action of the Holy Spirit even now acting in His Church.

We will profit more spiritually from the ineffable riches the Lord has placed at our disposal in the Liturgy of the Holy Mass when we know, love, and live it more wholeheartedly. The best way to do so is by participating fully, consciously, and actively in that bountiful liturgy.

141. What are the main parts of the "Liturgy of the Word" at Mass?

The "Liturgy of the Word" is the first major part of Mass. It includes:

a) the Old and New Testaments as well as a Responsorial Psalm—God's Word listened to;

b) Homily—God's Word explained;

c) Profession of Faith—God's Word accepted and held fast;

d) Prayer of the Faithful—God's Word appealed to.

In the readings, and especially the Gospel, Christ is present to His people in His Word.

142. What are the main parts of the "Liturgy of the Eucharist" at Mass?

The "Liturgy of the Eucharist" is the second major part of Mass. It includes:

a) the Preparation of the Gifts and their presentation;

b) the Eucharistic Prayer with its enactment at the Consecration and the offering of it to the Father;

c) and the Communion Rite by partaking of the sacrificial meal of Holy Communion.

At the Last Supper Christ instituted the Paschal Sacrifice and Meal. In this unique meal the Sacrifice of the Cross is continually made present in the Church when the priest, representing Christ, carries out precisely what the Lord did and handed over to His disciples to continually perform in His memory.

a) In the Preparation of the Gifts, the bread, wine, and water are brought to the altar, employing the very same elements which Christ used.

b) The Eucharistic Prayer is our hymn of thanksgiving to God for the whole work of salvation with the offerings becoming the very Body and Blood of our Savior.

c) The Breaking of Bread together is a sign of the, unity of the faithful who in Holy Communion receive the very Body and Blood, soul and divinity of Christ just as the Apostles did from the hands of their Master.

143. When do Priests change the bread into Christ's Sacred Body and the wine into His Precious Blood?

By the words of consecration, the priest changes the bread into the sacred Body of Jesus and the wine into His precious Blood.

After the consecration of the bread the priest holds the sacred Host aloft and then after he consecrates the wine he does the same with the chalice of the precious Blood so that we may adore Christ, our Lord. Gazing at the sacred Host and chalice, we may well offer a silent prayer, such as:

> "O Sacrament most holy
>
> O Sacrament divine,
>
> All praise and all thanksgiving
>
> Be every moment Thine."

Or we may simply gaze upon the consecrated species believingly while adoring silently and praying,

> "My Lord and my God!"

Gaining from Our Receiving of Holy Communion

144. What do we receive in Holy Communion?

In Holy Communion we receive the risen and glorified Body and Blood of our Lord Jesus Christ as our food for gaining eternal life, just as Communion indicates this profound union.

145. When did Christ command us to receive Holy Communion?

Christ commanded us to receive Holy Communion when He told us, "Amen, amen, I say to you, unless you eat the Flesh of the Son of Man and drink His Blood, you do not have life within you"(Jn 6:53).

146. What are the astoundingly great effects of our receiving of Holy Communion?

The astounding effects of receiving Holy Communion are:

a) that it brings us into the closest union with our Lord and increases sanctifying grace within us;

b) that it reduces our inclination toward evil and gives us the desire and strength to lead good Catholic lives;

c) that it remits venial sins and guards against mortal ones;

d) and that it is a pledge of our future resurrection and blessedness in heaven.

"Whoever eats My flesh and drinks My blood has eternal life, and I will raise him up on the last day" (Jn 6:54).

A person who would receive Communion unworthily and knowingly in unconfessed serious sin would not gain its benefits and, in fact, would sin by a sacrilege which, however, can be forgiven in a sincere confession.

147 How should we prepare for receiving Holy Communion worthily?

We should prepare for receiving Holy Communion as follows:

a) if we should happen to be in mortal sin, we must first make a good sacramental confession;

b) we should also be sorry for any venial sins, but we need not go to confession before receiving;

c) we should try to participate fully, consciously, and actively in Holy Mass.

We should abstain from food and liquids (water and medicine excepted) for an hour before receiving Holy Communion, and, naturally, as far as possible, we should be dressed such that it may show our respect for the Mass. Also, we should approach the Table of the Lord with proper reverence, hands and eyes guarded in devotion.

Jesus remains sacramentally present in the Holy Eucharist as long as the Sacred Species remain in the form of bread and the form of wine. When the Sacred Species cease to be, Christ's presence then also ceases to be present. However, scrupulousness is never necessary. All left-over consecrated Hosts are kept in a ciborium and placed in the tabernacle for people who come to pray and for bringing Holy Communion to the sick and elderly.

**RECONCILIATION
OR
PENANCE**

The Sacrament of Peace

What Going to Confession Means to Us

148. When did our Lord institute for us the peace-giving Sacrament of Reconciliation or Penance?

When our Lord, Jesus, gave to His Apostles and their successors the power to forgive sins, He instituted in His Church the peace-giving Sacrament of

Reconciliation or Penance. Thus the faithful who fall into sin after Baptism may be renewed in grace, reconciled with God, and united with the whole Church-community to share fully in all its blessings.

In this Sacrament of Reconciliation we can attain a personal encounter with Jesus Christ Who, through His priest, brings about within us: (a) restoration or increase of sanctifying grace, (b) peaceful union with Himself, (c) forgiveness of our sins, (d) remission of the eternal or temporal punishment due to sin, (e) helps to avoid sin in the future, (f) restoration of the merits of our good works, (g) reconciliation with the Church-community to share in its many blessings.

Since sin affects the life of the whole Church, not only that of the sinner, a sincere confession also reconciles the penitent to God but to one another as well. By the loving mystery of the divine will, we human beings are joined together by a supernatural solidarity wherein the sin of one person injures all the others just as the holiness of one benefits all the others. Accordingly, Penance always entails a reconciliation with our brothers and sisters in the Church-community without their realizing it.

A real conversion of heart carries with it sorrow for sin together with the firm resolve to lead a better life as expressed to the Church through the priest. We then say or do our assigned penance and try to amend our lives.

149. How can we be sure that Christ has commanded Catholics to confess their sins to a Priest?

We know that Christ commands us to confess our sins to the priest

a) from the teaching words of Jesus about forgiveness of sins

b) and from the constant belief and teaching of the Church about this Sacrament of Peace.

The principal parts of the rite of going to confession and also the key elements in the whole aspect of forgiveness are contrition for sins, confession of these sins, performing the assigned acts of penance, and the absolution by the priest. Priests can easily be very understanding, patient, and forgiving because they also can be tempted and their holy position itself calls on them to be kind and forgiving.

150. What is genuine Contrition?

Contrition being the most important act of the penitent is a heartfelt sorrow for sins committed along with a deep intention of trying not to sin in the future by avoiding bad occasions.

151. What is the chief difference between perfect and imperfect contrition?

Contrition is "perfect" when the motive derives from deep sorrow because of true love of God as the highest Good Whom we have offended, showing ingratitude for His many blessings to us.

Contrition is "imperfect" when it is based on motives still of faith but not exclusively out of love of God, which motive can be seen in the traditional Act of Contrition which proclaims, "I am sorry because I dread the loss of heaven and the pains of hell." This "imperfect contrition," however, is sufficient for forgiveness of sins in our confession.

The inner examination of conscience from the heart and the outer admission of sins in confession should be made in the light of God's great mercy, and not from over anxiousness or excessive worry. On the part of the penitents, confession should be with openness of heart to the priest-confessor.

On the part of the confessor-priests is required a spiritual judgment by which, acting in the person of Christ and in the light of the Church's power to bind or loose, they should pronounce their decision of forgiveness or retention of sins only in the light of the penitents' sorrow for sins committed not the gravity of the sins which they confess. Besides, priests consistently presume such repentance from the mere fact that the penitents have come to them for absolution from their sins.

Indeed, the priest is compelled to give that absolution whenever the penitent seems truly sorry. In fact, basically, priests are not shocked over what or how grave may be the actual sins confessed so long as repentance for these sins is evident. Jesus Christ is really all that matters.

God uses visible signs to foster salvation among His people and to renew any battered covenant between Himself and one of His Catholics. Through the fact and the sign of absolution from the priest to the penitent in the name of Christ's Church, God thereby grants His pardon to respective sinners who in sacramental Confession manifest their sorrow and intention to strive to improve.

By means of the Sacrament of Reconciliation or Penance, God the Father welcomes the persons who want to come back to Him. And Christ symbolically places the formerly lost sheep on His own shoulders and brings it back to the sheepfold. Then the Holy Spirit returns to sanctify continually His very own temple or to dwell more fully in it. All of this is manifested by a renewed sharing in the Lord's table of the Mass and then there is great joy at the banquet of God's Church over the return of the person who had formerly been rather lost and wandering.

152. Who really forgives our sins through the absolution of the priest?

Through His divine mercy it is God alone Who forgives sins using His ordained priests to grant absolution in His place and His name.

The Church thereby becomes the instrument of forgiveness through the priest's absolution and of the conversion of penitents through the ministry entrusted by our Lord to the Apostles, to their successors, and to priests.

The priest's role is to fulfill his office of judge of the penitent's contrition wisely. He should be grateful that he has been chosen to absolve from repentant sins of all sorts and forms and to be very kind to those who come before him for confession.

The more that priests absolve from big sins the more merit they will receive in heaven. Besides, as long as we are sorry for our sins, there is really nothing to fear from the priest. In fact, priests are happy that people are coming to them for absolution from their sins.

153. What are the usual steps when going to Confession?

The usual steps in the Sacrament of Reconciliation are:

a) making a sincere but peaceful examination of conscience recalling the nature and approximate number of times any mortal sin was committed;

b) accepting the reception that the priest extends with a reading of Scripture or the saying of some prayers;

c) confessing one's sins humbly and as thoroughly as possible;

d) listening to the kindly advice given by the priest and accepting the penance he assigns;

e) making a sincere act of contrition together with receiving the absolution of the priest;

f) and finally, leaving to go out and perform one's assigned penance while giving thanks to our kind, merciful, and loving Lord, Jesus.

Before celebrating the Sacrament of Reconciliation or Penance, both the penitent and the priest ought to prepare themselves by prayer and possibly some fasting. The Confessors might well call upon the Holy Spirit for light, leniency, and mercifulness. Penitents might well examine their consciences peacefully yet fully in the light of God's Commandments and the Church's Precepts, then pray to the Lord for forgiveness and courage and peace.

During the examination of conscience the penitent should recall that he or she is in God's presence from whom nothing can or ought to be hidden. In this relaxed atmosphere the preparation for confession ought not become an agony, but, rather, a release, recalling that the Lord is infinitely merciful, compassionate, and even tender. Also, whatever may have inadvertently been left unsaid in the actual confessing of sins should thereafter be forgotten and left to the mercy of the Sacred Heart. However, should something bother a person, it can always be mentioned in the next confession.

154. What should we confess in the Sacrament of Penance?

We should confess all grave sins with their approximate number of times together with any extraordinary circumstances which may have attended them. Venial sins may also be confessed without any exaggerations.

Confession restores the complete life of the soul, all merit from good works, the removal of punishments due to any sins, along with great peace.

(For a prayer of contrition, see "Basic Catholic Prayers," p. 158.)

We can go to confession anywhere and almost at any time or place such as in the Church confessional, in a hospital, auto, rectory, home, or while walking. Confessions may be made with anonymity or face to face, but always with respect.

The Priest in Confession

155. How serious is the Seal of Confession binding every priest-confessor?

The seal of confession is the sacred obligation seriously imposed on all priest-confessors never, under any circumstances whatsoever, to reveal anything made known to them in any confession.

There is no known instance of any priest ever violating the sacredly tight-bound seal of confession by revealing anything whatsoever heard in a confession, not even by any priest who may have abandoned the practice of his priesthood whatever may have been his souring experience or disillusionment. On the other hand, there are numerous cases on record in which a priest went to his death rather than reveal what had been told to him in any confession.

The seal of confession is absolute and completely binding on each and every priest by solemn vow to God almighty. That seal applies under each and every circumstance, even should that confession be invalid or absolution be denied. The confessor is seriously forbidden never to say to anyone anything whatsoever, including even to the penitent outside of confession. No one, not even a Pope, can under any pretext, however important, ever attempt to dispense any priest from the complete secrecy of the Seal of Confession. Nor may the confessor treat the penitent any differently, even after he or she dies, because of what he may have learned from any penitent in Confession.

Clearly, God watches in a special way over this Seal of Confession and its scrupulous observance, so that the faithful can go to Confession certain that nothing will ever be revealed about their sins from their confession.

156. What is a partial and a plenary Indulgence?

An indulgence is the remission of some or all of the temporal punishment due to sins, which debt may yet remain after the sins are forgiven. It is that punishment which must be satisfied either on earth or in purgatory.

This applies because of our transgression even after that sin has been forgiven by the absolution of a priest. As all Catholics know, the penance given by the priest in confession is really rather slight, actually a few simple prayers leaving the penitent free to do anything more on his or her own.

A *plenary* indulgence is a release from all punishment due to absolved sin, whereas a *partial* indulgence is a release from some of such.

ANOINTING OF THE SICK OR AGED

The Sacrament of Peaceful Anticipation

What This Sacrament Is and
Does for Our Sick and Aged

157. *What is the Sacrament of the Anointing of the Sick?*

The Sacrament of the Anointing of the Sick is the Sacrament for Catholics who are seriously ill as a result of some sickness or old age. Through it Christ strengthens the faithful who are afflicted by any illness, providing them with the strongest means of support.

Suffering and illness have always been among the greatest problems to challenge the human spirit. Christians experience pain as do all people; yet their faith helps them to grasp more fully the mystery of the "whys" and to bear their pain more bravely. From the words of Jesus they realize that their sickness can have meaning and value such as toward their own salvation and that of the world. They also know that Jesus loves the sick and that during His life He often visited and healed the sick.

158. *What are the three distinct aspects of administering the Sacrament of the Anointing of the Sick?*

The three distinct aspects of this sacrament are:

a) the prayer of faith,

b) the laying on of hands,

c) and the anointing with holy oil especially blessed by the bishop on Holy Thursday.

The Prayer of Faith. The community, asking God's help for the sick, makes its prayer of faith in response to the Lord's Word and in a deep spirit of trust. It is the people of Christ who pray in faith during these rites for the sick. Even the entire Church is made present and praying together for those being anointed. And if they are able, the sick persons should certainly also join in this prayer of faith.

The Laying on of Hands. The Gospels contain a number of instances in which Jesus healed the sick by laying on His hands or even by some simple gesture as a mere touch. With this gesture of laying on his hands, the priest thereby indicates that this particular person now being anointed is the object of the Church's prayer of faith for healing. The laying on of hands is clearly a sign seeking a blessing as all present pray that by Christ's healing power the sick persons may be restored to health or at least become strengthened to withstand the illness. The laying on of hands also indicates that the Church is praying for the coming of the Holy Spirit upon the sick person. Above all this laying on of hands is a biblical gesture of healing.

The Anointing with Holy Oil. The practice of anointing the sick with blessed oil signifies both healing (Mk 6:13) and strengthening (Jas 5:14) as well as the presence of the Spirit. Then the sick person is anointed on the forehead and on the hands with the form:

> "Through this holy anointing
> may the Lord in His love and mercy
> help you with the grace of the Holy Spirit.
> May the Lord Who frees you from sin
> save you and raise you up."

Then the sick or elderly persons and those in attendance respond "Amen" in fervent appeal to the divine Healer.

Just a prudent or probable judgment about the seriousness of the sickness is sufficient. In such a case there is no reason for scruples, but if necessary a doctor may be consulted.

HOLY ORDERS

**The Sacrament of the Great Gift
to Our Priests**

**What this Sacrament Is and
Does for Our Priests**

159. What is the Sacrament of Holy Orders?

Holy Orders is the Sacrament by which the office of bishop, priest, or deacon is conferred on certain men together with its powers and graces.

The outward sign of the Sacrament of Holy Orders is the laying on of hands and the accompanying prayer by the bishop along with other ceremonies.

160. How do we know for certain that Jesus Christ instituted the Sacrament of Holy Orders?

**We know that Jesus Christ instituted the Sacrament of Holy Orders
a) from Sacred Scripture
b) and from the constant teaching of the Church throughout her entire history.**

Christ our Lord Himself bestowed on the Apostles the grace and the powers of His sacred Priesthood at the Last Supper, and afterward the Apostles also handed on this power to others as priests.

"I remind you to fan into flame the gift of God that is within you through the laying on of my hands" (2 Tim 1:6).

The Apostles understood their office as a priestly one, as a participation in the very priesthood of Jesus Christ. Primarily, this office of the priests consists in building up the Church, by continuing the priestly mission of Christ in word, in Sacraments, and in being a living example. In this sense every priest is a representative of Christ, and this position has great significance especially for celebrating the Holy Eucharist.

The Powers Conferred on Our Priests

161. What does Ordination do for men who are newly ordained priests?

a) Priestly ordination imprints the souls of the men being ordained with an indelible or unremovable mark of the sacred priesthood;

b) it bestows the powers to offer the Holy Sacrifice of the Mass for the living and for the dead;

c) it increases sanctifying grace;

d) and it strengthens the newly ordained priest to live a good priestly life, fulfill his priestly duties, and attain eternal salvation.

As long as there are human beings on this earth, the spiritual ministry for which, primarily, the priest is ordained will always be needed and wanted. Indeed, there is scarcely a more meaningful, a more satisfying, and a more important work to which a person can be dedicated than to proclaim the Lord's available salvation as one of His priests.

Any capable youth who feels that he or she may possibly have some God-inspired desire to think a bit further about how to be admitted into a seminary to prepare to become a priest or brother or into a convent to become a Sister should pray over it, then consult a wise priest.

**Vocations to the
Priesthood Today**

He will advise such a generous young person to attempt it only if that priest truly discerns a likely vocation from the Lord to follow such a privileged calling.

Some Saints have claimed that the highest degree possible of happiness on this earth depends on following the will of God, wherever it may lead. In addition, provided that there is a call from Jesus to follow Him more closely, then eternal life in heaven would await such a person after a fulfilled life with many friends.

The need is great; God's grace is assured; the Church is waiting for the generous and courageous response of those youths called to this glorious life of love and service.

162. Why do Catholic Priests of the Latin Rite live celibate, unmarried lives?

Catholic priests live celibate lives in order to give themselves, their time, and their efforts more fully to God's people as ordained priests.

Also, Church authorities have long required Latin Rite priests to live and work as chaste, unmarried, and consecrated men.

Priests are loving people who strongly cultivate a deep personal union with our Lord Jesus and with our heavenly Blessed Mother both of whom assist priests to lead pure and chaste lives while having many friends in their productive lives.

Laypeople Also Share in the Priesthood of Christ

163. How does the Ministerial Priesthood of ordained Priests differ from the Universal Priesthood of the Catholic laity?

The universal priesthood of the faithful is their way of participating in the priesthood of Christ for the salvation of all. It is, however, different in essence and not only in degree from the ministerial priesthood.

"Like living stones, let yourselves be built up into a spiritual temple and become a holy priesthood to offer spiritual sacrifices acceptable to God through Jesus Christ. . . . You are 'a chosen race, a royal priesthood, a holy nation, a people claimed by God as His Own possession,' so that you may proclaim the glorious deeds of Him Who called you out of darkness into His marvelous light" (1 Pet 2:5-9).

MATRIMONY

The Sacrament of
Togetherness Throughout Life

God Instituted Marriage and
Christ Elevated It to a Sacrament

164. Who started Marriage and who raised it to be a Holy Sacrament?

God instituted or began marriage and Christ raised it to a Sacrament called Holy Matrimony.

"For this reason a man shall leave his father and mother and be joined to his wife, and the two shall become one flesh. This is a great mystery. Here I am applying it to Christ and the Church" (Eph 5:31-32).

The Council of Trent reaffirmed that marriage in the Church is indeed one of the great seven Sacraments instituted by Christ Himself. In fact, the Church is the guardian of Holy Matrimony, constantly upholding the unity, dignity, and sacredness of this holy union right up until either of the spouses dies.

What This Sacrament Is and
Does for Our Marrying Couple

165. What happens to the marrying couple in the Sacrament of Matrimony?

In the Sacrament of Matrimony

a) Christ joins a loving man and woman in a holy and indissoluble union,

b) He enables them to signify and to share in the mystery of that great unity and fruitful love which exists between Christ and His Church,

c) and He gives them both all of the graces needed to fulfill their tasks both as husband and wife together and as parents raising their children as good Catholics.

"Jesus replied, 'Have you not read that from the beginning the Creator "made them male and female" and said: "That is why a man leaves his father and mother and is joined to his wife, and the two become one flesh"? And so they are no longer two but one flesh' "(Mt 19:4-6).

"God created man in love to share His divine life. We see His high destiny in the love of husband and wife, which bears the imprint of God's own divine love. Love is man's origin, love is his calling, love is his fulfillment in heaven. The love of man and woman is made holy in the Sacrament of Matrimony, and it becomes the mirror of God's everlasting love" (From the Preface to the Nuptial Mass).

166. What do the Bride and Groom declare in the presence of the authorized priest and two witnesses?

The bride and groom declare in the presence of the authorized priest and two witnesses that they take each other as husband and wife "for better or for worse until death do us part."

The couple to be married should first obtain a marriage license from the civil authorities after having their blood test. Some countries might also require a civil marriage, but this does not exempt the couple from the grave obligation to be married by a Catholic priest. In the eyes of the Church, Catholics are not married until they are properly married "in the Church," which means in the presence of an authorized Catholic priest. Also, although the Rite of Matrimony does give reluctant approval in special circumstances for a marriage to take place outside of a nuptial Mass, a truly Catholic marriage should certainly be celebrated with a uniting Mass wherein the marriage-ceremony takes place just after the Liturgy of the Word.

167. What are some lasting effects of receiving the Sacrament of Matrimony?

Some lasting effects of receiving the Sacrament of Matrimony are:

a) it increases sanctifying grace within the bride and groom,

b) it gives the married couple the special graces to remain faithful to their bond of marriage until death, dutifully fulfilling obligations together,

c) and it also imparts those graces required for the Christian upbringing of the children whom God has entrusted to their care.

168. What basically should married persons do to preserve their marriage?

Married persons should

a) live together in love, harmony, support in utter faithfulness;

b) help strengthen and encourage each other to live good Catholic lives;

c) and bring up their children in the love and wholesome fear of the Lord as good practicing Catholics.

Certainly also parents should help to prepare their children for life in the world by helping them toward obtaining the education and training to get started in the world, while overseeing each one's religious education.

169. Can a truly valid marriage ever really be dissolved?

A truly valid marriage cannot really be dissolved.

"What God has joined together, let no one separate" (Mt. 19:6). "Anyone who divorces his wife and marries another commits adultery, and anyone who marries a woman divorced from her husband commits adultery" (Lk 16:18).

When the State or judge grants a civil divorce thereby breaking a valid marriage and then permits the divorced persons to marry again, this has no validity in the eyes of the Lord. For serious reasons the Church may permit a Catholic married couple to live apart temporarily hoping for a reconciliation to come back together again. But really divorced Catholics are not free to enter into another marriage in the Church. Of course, Catholics are not free to do things just because they are "legal" but outside of the will of Christ or of His Church.

It is possible, nevertheless, that a seeming marriage was really invalid from the beginning because of a serious impediment, which may or may not have been known to the couple originally.

Then after due process at the chancery through the parish priest, with much careful study of facts completed, Church authorities can declare that an annulment exists with no original bond any longer in effect; hence both parties are free to remarry.

Preparing for Marriage

170. What is expected of those who want to enter into a sacramental marriage?

Those who want to enter into marriage are expected to

a) be free of all impediments to marriage,

b) become engaged only after sufficient acquaintance with each other, and possibly after consulting their parents (also, they should try to let the priest who is to officiate know about six months before the wedding day is to be set);

c) and go to Confession and receive Holy Communion, possibly together, in view of their pending marriage.

Some impediments to marriage are: a prior valid marriage, too close a degree of blood relationship, lack of age, not having a civil license, or a difference of religion. Some, known as "impeding" impediments, can be waived by Church authorities where there is sufficient reason. Others, known as "diriment" impediments, are incompatible with the very nature of marriage and can never be set aside such as a prior marriage with the spouse still living.

Mixed Marriages—as between a Catholic and a non-Catholic—may reluctantly be permitted with a dispensation from Church authorities. But mixed marriages are to be discouraged as probably only second best. This is so because in many cases the marriage of a Catholic to a non-Catholic can easily give rise to serious, if not insoluble, difficulties. It is especially difficult for spouses of different religions to be able really to pray together or attend Mass regularly and united.

(For useful questions on the above chapter, see pp. 147-149.)

The blessed Sacramental things of life rise to heaven and return with an odor of sanctity.

XV.
THE SACRAMENTALS—
MANY LITTLE BLESSINGS

171. What are Sacramentals?

Sacramentals are sacred signs or blessed objects which signify effects, particularly of a spiritual nature, which are obtained for us through the intercession of the Church, through the use of which various occasions and things in life are rendered more helpful and holy.

172. How do Sacramentals differ from the Sacraments?

Sacramentals differ from the Sacraments in that they were not directly instituted by Christ as the Sacraments were. They do not produce grace of themselves as the Sacraments do, and are not signs of Christ's direct actions on our souls as the Sacraments are. Sacramentals were instituted by the Church over the years and they obtain graces for us only indirectly, that is, by arousing fervent acts of virtue which may certainly help to win God's graces and blessings on us, provided they are u⸓ as intended.

Effects of Using
the Sacramentals

173. *To obtain what blessings do Catholics make use of Sacramentals?*

The chief effects obtained by using the Sacramentals are:

a) the granting from God of some actual graces to help us,

b) the forgiveness of venial sins,

c) the remission of temporal punishments due to our sins,

d) the increased health of body,

e) the granting of material blessings for our real earthly lives,

f) and the acquisition of a more spiritual outlook on the use of several ordinary things, thereby uplifting their use and enjoyment.

174. *Which are the chief kinds of Sacramentals?*

The chief kinds of Sacramentals are: blessings of various kinds, exorcisms and blessed objects of devotion. The most frequently used objects for use as Sacramentals after they have been blessed as such are: Holy Water, ashes, candles, palms, crucifixes, statues, rosary beads, scapulars, and images of Jesus, Mary, Joseph, and many other Saints.

The main purpose of the Church's blessings on Sacramentals is to invoke God's favor and blessings on certain persons, places, and things. Some examples of these are: Benediction of the Blessed Sacrament, blessing of the sick, of fields, of harvests, of automobiles or boats, as well as the blessing of children and youths by their parents.

Blessed articles ought to be treated with reverence, in a spirit of faith, and trusting in God's goodness for the blessings we desire.

175. For what purposes, for instance, do Catholics use Holy Water?

We Catholics use Holy Water, usually making the sign of the Cross, to ask for God's blessings, and to help ward off the evil from ills of body and soul.

Holy Water is used as a reminder of baptismal water and our baptismal promises made in our name by our godparents. Catholic homes might well make good use of Holy Water as a popular Sacramental with many uses in the home.

(For useful questions on the above chapter, see p. 149.)

VALUABLE APPENDICES

Since the appendices in many books seem musty with lists of books and other less attractive materials, none was originally intended here. But the present appendices seemed so valuable that they simply had to be offered for your benefit.

a) Useful Questions for Each Chapter—help the readers to review each chapter in order to make sure they have gotten the best out of each. There is no attempt to make any question tricky; in fact, they are to the point and quite easy.

b) Summary of Chief Vatican II Messages—may seem like a monumental offering, but, since the author has published two outstanding books on the Second Vatican Council, he was able to present in brief what he considers the best and most practical of Vatican II's messages for busy people.

c) Basic Catholic Prayers—are just that; basic, minimal but essential.

(A)
USEFUL QUESTIONS FOR EACH CHAPTER

The numbers in parentheses after each question give the numbers of the doctrinal points treated within this book and these show where the answers to the following Useful Questions can easily be found.

I. *What Religion Is:*

What is the relationship between human beings and God? (1)

How can human beings gain eternal salvation? (2)

II. *Divine Revelation:*

Why must we believe what God has revealed? (3)

What is the Bible? (4)

What does "covenant" mean in a religious sense? (5)

What is the New Testament? (6)

What does "inspiration of the Bible" mean? (7)

What does "biblical inerrancy" mean? (8)

Name the main points which each of the Gospel writers wants to establish. (9)

What is Sacred Church Tradition? (10)

What three sources combine to bring us God's revelation? (11)

With what mentality should Catholics read the Bible (12)

III. *One God in Three Persons:*

Say the Apostles' Creed. (13)
Who is God? (14)
How do we know that God exists? (15)
Name some perfections of God. (16)
What is the Most Blessed Trinity? (17)
Why does God permit some evil in our world? (18)

IV. *God the Supreme Creator:*

What are Angels? (19)
What are Evil Spirits? (20)
When does God breathe forth an immortal soul for a human being? (21)

V. *Original and Personal Sin:*

What is Original sin? (23)
What, in general, are the ways of committing personal sins? (25)
Name the three conditions for committing a mortal sin. (26)
Name the seven capital sins. (27)

VI. *Christ Our Lord and Redeemer:*

Why did Jesus Christ become man? (28)
How do we know that Christ is the promised Messiah (29)
How did Jesus Christ prove that He was God? (30)
What does Christ's Resurrection mean? (31)
What does Christ's Resurrection prove to us? (32)

VII. *The Holy Spirit and God's Helpful Grace:*

How does God's actual grace help us? (35)
What chief grace does God give to everyone? (36)
What does Sanctifying Grace help us to become? (37)

VIII. *Holiness of Life:*

Name the three theological and the four moral virtues. (38)
Name the eight Beatitudes. (39)
Who is the best Person to imitate for Christian perfection? (40)
Name some chief means for attaining Christian perfection. (41)
Explain the three Evangelical Counsels. (42)

IX. *Our Catholic Church:*

How did God prepare for the founding of Christ's Church? (43)

What basically is the Catholic Church? (44)

What is the Pope? (45)

What is a General Council of the Church? (47)

What is a Papal Encyclical? (48)

What is a priest? (50)

Name the four distinctive marks of the Catholic Church. (51)

What three powers did Christ give to His Church? (52)

When is the Pope infallible? (53)

Why is the Catholic Church called, "The Church of Salvation"? (54)

X. *Our Blessed Mother and the Saints:*

Name some prerogatives of the Blessed Virgin Mary. (55)

Why is Mary rightly called, "The Mother of God"? (56)

What did Pope Paul VI urge about devotion to our Blessed Mother? (57)

Who is St. Joseph? (58)

Who belong to the Communion of Saints? (59)

How does the honor we give to Saints differ from the honor we pay to God? (60)

How can we help the Souls in Purgatory? (61)

Why does Purgatory seem logically proper? (62)

XI. *Christ's and Our Resurrection in Heaven:*

When did Jesus ascend to Heaven? (63)
What does "Jesus sits at the right hand of the Father Almighty" mean? (64)
What basically happens in human death? (65)
What takes place soon after a person dies? (66)
What will happen at our own resurrection? (67)
What are some basic joys in heaven? (68)
What souls go to Purgatory and why? (70)
How do we know that there is an eternal Hell for those who blamingly become damned there? (71)
What and why is the General Judgment? (72)

XII. *God's Ten Commandments:*

What is a person's conscience? (74)
How can we show our love for God? (76)
How can we love ourselves correctly? (77)
Give reasons why we should love all people. (79)
Name God's ten Commandments. (81)
What does the first Commandment require? (82)
How can people sin against faith? (83)
What should we do to preserve our faith? (84)
What does the second Commandment forbid? (85)
What does the third Commandment require of Catholics? (86)
What does the fourth Commandment require of everyone? (87)
What does the fourth Commandment require of children? (88)

How can children sin against their parents or lawful superiors? (90)

What does the fifth Commandment forbid? (92)

How do we sin against the respect due to ourselves? (95)

How can we sin against the respect due to others? (96)

What must one do if he or she has harmed the soul or body of another? (97)

What does God forbid in the sixth and ninth Commandments? (98)

Name some aids to preserve sexual purity. (99)

What should persons think about when they are sexually tempted? (100)

What do the seventh and tenth Commandments forbid? (101)

When does a person sin against another person's belongings? (102)

How can a person sin by cooperating in a sin of theft by another? (103)

What must people do who have sinned against the money or belongings of someone else? (104)

What does the eighth Commandment forbid? (105)

When does speech become a sin against the person or name or character of another? (106)

XIII. *The Precepts of the Church:*

Name the seven Precepts of the Catholic Church for the United States. (108)

What does the first Precept about Mass require of Catholics? (109)

Name the American Catholic Holy Days. (110)

Name the chief seasons of the Church's Liturgical Year. (111)

What does the second Precept about Confession and Holy Communion require of us? (112)

Name some conditions for receiving Holy Communion worthily. (113)

What does the third Precept about religious education require of Catholics? (114)

What should Catholics do to prepare for the Sacrament of Matrimony according to the fourth Precept? (115)

In what ways can Catholics support the Church as in the fifth Precept? (116)

What does the sixth Precept about doing penances ask of us? (117)

What does the seventh Precept on the Church's Apostolate request of all Catholics? (120)

XIV. *Christ's Seven Sacraments and the Mass:*

What in general is a Sacrament? (121)

Name the seven Sacraments. (122)

What does Baptism do for a person? (123)

Why is Baptism known as the most fundamental Sacrament? (124)

Name some effective fruits of Baptism. (125)

What does the indelible mark on the soul from Baptism indicate? (126)

What does Confirmation do for those confirmed? (127)

Name some effects of receiving Confirmation. (128)

What is the Holy Eucharist? (130)

When did Jesus institute the Holy Eucharist? (131)

How do we know that Jesus Christ is truly present in the Holy Eucharist? (133)

Why is our Mass the sacrifice of the New Covenant and what does this mean? (135)

How can we Catholics best celebrate the Mass? (138)

Why does the Mass also instruct us? (140)

Name the main parts in the "Liturgy of the Word" at Mass. (141)

Name the main parts in the "Liturgy of the Eucharist." (142)

Name some outstanding effects of receiving Holy Communion. (146)

How should we prepare for receiving Holy Communion? (147)

When did Jesus give His priests the awesome power to forgive sins in His Name? (148)

How do we know that Jesus wants us to confess our sins through priests in His Name? (149)

What is the most important possession of Catholics while going to Confession? (150)

What is the main difference between perfect and imperfect contrition? (151)

Name the steps in going to Confession. (153)

What should we confess in the Sacrament of Reconciliation or Penance? (154)

What is the Seal of Confession and how binding is it on the father-confessor? (155)

What is the meaning of an indulgence? (156)

What are the three distinctive aspects while the Anointing of the Sick is being administered? (158)

What is the Sacrament of Holy Orders? (159)

How do we know that Jesus Christ Himself instituted the sharing in His Sacred Priesthood by Catholic priests throughout the world, and through the centuries? (160)

What graces does the ordination of a man empower him to do and to be? (161)

Why do Catholic priests live celibate unmarried lives? (162)

Since Catholic laypeople also share in the Priesthood of Christ, how then do priests and the laity differ in sharing this? (163)

What happens to a man and woman when a couple becomes united in the holy Sacrament of Matrimony? (165)

How should Catholic couples prepare for marriage? (170)

XV. The Sacramentals:

What are Sacramentals? (171)

How chiefly do Sacramentals differ from the Sacraments? (172)

Why do we Catholics make use of the Sacramentals? (173)

Name some most frequently used objects which are blessed to become Sacramentals. (174)

Valuable Appendices:

(B) Give your opinion of the usefulness of the Summary of Vatican II's Messages (p. 150).

(C) Could you name some prayers which you would like to be included in the Basic Catholic Prayers? (p. 156)

(B)
SUMMARY OF CHIEF VATICAN II MESSAGES

The great Second Vatican Council has been called by Pope John Paul II "an outstanding milestone in the 2,000 year history of our Holy Church."

While their importance is well known, the actual messages of the Council's documents either may not have been read by many or may have been misunderstood or exaggerated or minimized. It was deemed important, therefore, to include this Summary of Vatican II teachings in this book.

The following outline summary of all major Vatican II messages was originally presented by the author in Rome to a group of 180 select people from several countries throughout the world.

The chapter titles and the Vatican II passage numbers refer to the book, CATHOLIC LIVING TODAY, Hope from Vatican II, by Rev. R. Fullam, S.J. and published in 1981 by Catholic Book Publishing Co., New

York. Any reliable book of Vatican II documents will use the same officially-numbered passages as given here.

The reader will note how traditional are the points of the great Council and yet how needed are the emphases on Renewal, Commitment, Unity, and Witness for the advancement of the Catholic Church in our times.

In order to derive the choicest fruits from this summary, it is recommended that each point be pondered for tasting the spiritual flavor. The implications for our world-wide Church of various age groups of God's people in many diverse cultures of our planet may easily be discerned.

The following summary is taken from the book *Catholic Living Today—Hope from Vatican II.*

THE RENEWAL OF CATHOLICS

FOR CHRIST'S GOALS

Chapter 1. *Responding to God's Call to Be His People Today*
A) The Church is deeply concerned for man's well-being. (World: 3, 11)
B) Scripture shows God's interest today in man's life. (World: 41; Revelation: 4, 6)
C) Living today as the community of God's people. (Church: 9, 13, 16)

Chapter 2. *Rejecting God and Religion Loses Life's Best Meaning*
A) Understanding the causes of atheism and irreligion. (World: 19, 20)
B) Christians should share dialogue and love with all. (World: 7, 21)

Chapter 3. *Integrating Wisely the Sacred and Worldly in Life*
A) Forging peaceful living by following God's Norms. (World: 15, 43; Church: 36)
B) Life is benefited temporally and eternally by Christian living. (World: 42, 44, 53, 54)

Chapter 4. *Shunning Sin in Today's World for Human Dignity*
A) True dignity spurns sin by following conscience. (World: 16, 17, 30)
B) Respect for human beings requires their just treatment. (World: 27, 29, 31, 63)

Chapter 5. *Aiming toward heaven's blessedness forever in Christ*
A) Heaven's new life with Christ and loved ones. (World: 18, 39; Church: 48)
B) Enhancing earthly life before joining heaven's saints. (World: 57; Church: 49)

THE COMMITMENT OF CATHOLICS TO CHRIST'S CAUSE

Chapter 6. *Protecting a fair climate for Religious Freedom*
A) Human dignity deserves freedom from coercion. (Freedom: 2, 3,11)
B) Religious freedom can even be conducive to religion's practice. (Freedom: 3, 8)

Chapter 7. *Providing spiritual life by Christ's presence in His Church*
A) The unfolding mystery and reality of Christ's Kingdom. (Church: 5, 7)
B) The Catholic Faith offers Christ's fullness of revelation. (Church: 8; Missions: 7)

Chapter 8. *Sharing together in Christ's powerful blessings*
A) Priests and laypersons help sanctify, teach, and guide. (Church: 34, 35, 36, 37)
B) The service offered by bishops, priests, and religious. (Church: 22; Bishops: 16; Priests: 9; Seminaries: 19; Religious: 2)

Chapter 9. *Performing apostolic works locally and in the world*
A) All are called to zealous activity as capable. (Laity: 2, 8, 12, 33)
B) Spreading Christ's cause in all of life's circumstances. (Church: 31; Laity: 10, 11, 16, 18, 29)
C) Mission spirit shows our vitality requiring best means. (Missions: 1, 9; Communications: 1, 3)

THE UNITY OF CATHOLICS BY CHRIST'S WAYS

Chapter 10. *Following the way of holiness throughout life's quest*
A) Everyone is called by Christ to sanctify all of life. (Church: 40, 41)
B) Christ and His Church assist us all to acquire holiness. (Church: 39, 42, 50; Laity: 4)

Chapter 11. *Growing in Jesus through Mass, Communion, and all Sacraments*
A) Full participation with Christ at Mass and Communion. (Liturgy: 2, 7, 14; Laity: 8)
B) Advancing by the strength of Christ's Sacraments. (Liturgy: 12, 39, 122; Church: 11)

Chapter 12. *Gaining in life with our Blessed Mother's help*
A) Mary's prerogatives enable her to help people. (Church: 65, 66)
B) True devotion to our Lady fosters following of Christ. (Church: 60, 67, 69)

Chapter 13. *Reaching as united Christians for Christ's desired goals.*
A) The need for unity among Christian sects soon. (Ecumenism: 1, 3; World: 42)
B) Recommendations for unity of Western and Eastern Churches. (Ecumenism: 4,9; Easterns: 3, 27)

THE WITNESS OF CATHOLICS
IN CHRIST'S WORLD

Chapter 14. Discerning Christ's deliverance from tensions of the times
A) Analyzing wisely the conclusions in modern life. (World: 4, 5, 7, 8)
B) Religious insight sees beyond mere superficial progress. (World: 37, 43, 44; Laity: 12, 14)

Chapter 15. *Striving for an improved world by goodwilled people*
A) A better world for human living is possible. (World: 23, 24,84,88)
B) God-respecting people can unite for mankind's improvement. (Non Christians: 1, 2, 5; World: 42)

Chapter 16. *Crystallizing unity and sanctity in marriage and family*
A) Loving spouses fully sharing as husband and wife. (World: 48,50)
B) The Christian family, school of humanity and vestibule to heaven. (World: 51, 52)

Chapter 17. *Cherishing Catholic formation of our children and youth*
A) Guiding stars for educating our younger Catholics. (Education: 1, 3, 7)
B) Hopeful prospects for our nobly maturing youth. (Education: 2, 5, 8)

Chapter 18. *Promoting dignity and justice for socioeconomic order*

A) Principles for guiding business and all gainful work. (World: 63, 64, 67).

B) Guidelines toward establishing proper socio-economic conditions. (World: 70, 72)

Chapter 19. *Invigorating the common good on the national scene*

A) Stability and right order within the national community. (World: 74)

B) Smooth relations between authorities of Government and Church. (World: 76)

Chapter 20. *Exploring prospects for international harmony with hope*

A) Desired peace begins by serious efforts toward justice. (World: 77, 78, 79, 81, 82)

B) United in God, people can have good reasons for hope. (World: 24, 38, 89, 90)

CONCLUDING REMARKS.

We must truly pray for wisdom and trust in the guidance of the Holy Spirit behind the Second Vatican Council. For it planted the seeds which must be cultivated during the 1980's so that the harvest may soon be plentiful. For the current trends within Catholicism today will affect the lives of people for many generations to come.

The present Vatican Council II era of the 1980's will, undoubtedly, not have the very last word in the development of the dynamic gospel message or the ever-current Church of Christ. These enlightening messages do offer, however, the contemporary applications of the gospel for Catholics in modern times. The present era offers great opportunity to be truly alive in Christ and to glimpse the vision of tomorrow by expanding the Vatican II Church of today.

Our Creator's world is opening up vast new horizons of hope for our own age and for the future generations. The betterment and salvation of mankind, especially by Catholics who strive to live their religious faith in love within the light of our hope-filled Church of today, is all the more to the greater glory of God through Christ Jesus.

(C)

BASIC CATHOLIC PRAYERS

"I call you My friends" our Lord said at His Last Supper with us in mind. To deepen your personal, individual union with Jesus is to love our Lord more dearly within yourself.

When you say your prayers calmly with affection, it should help you to grow in prayer somewhat like the Apostles did, while praying with Jesus.

You will need help, direction, and strength in order to grow spiritually inside yourself. But you also, certainly, can feel with St. Augustine that, "what other Catholics before you have done, you can do today." So, just talk with Jesus and you'll feel your love and power growing.

The Sign of the Cross

In the Name of the Father,
and of the Son,
and of the Holy Spirit. Amen.

The Morning Offering

O Jesus,
through the immaculate heart of Mary,
I offer You
my prayers, works, joys, and sufferings
of this day
in union with the Holy Sacrifice of the Mass
through the world.

I offer them for all the intentions
of Your Sacred Heart;
the salvation of souls,
reparation for sin,
the reunion of all Christians.

I offer them
for the intentions of our Bishops
and of all members of the Apostleship of Prayers,
and in particular
for those recommended by our Holy Father this
month. Amen.

The Our Father

Our Father, Who art in heaven
hallowed be Thy Name;
Thy kingdom come;
Thy will be done on earth
as it is in heaven.
Give us this day our daily bread;
and forgive us our trespasses
as we forgive those who trespass against us;
and lead us not into temptation,
but deliver us from evil. Amen.

The Hail Mary

Hail, Mary,
full of grace,
the Lord is with you.
Blessed are you among women,
and blessed is the fruit of your womb, Jesus.
Holy Mary,
Mother of God,
pray for us sinners,
now and at the hour of our death. Amen.

The Glory Be to the Father

Glory be to the Father,
and to the Son,
and to the Holy Spirit:
as it was in the beginning,
is now,
and will be forever. Amen.

Act of Faith

O my God,
I firmly believe that You are one God
in three Divine Persons,
the Father, the Son, and the Holy Spirit.

I believe in Jesus Christ, Your Son,
Who became man and died for our sins,
and Who will come to judge
the living and the dead.
I believe these and all the truths
which the Holy Catholic Church teaches,
because You have revealed them,
Who can neither deceive nor be deceived. Amen.

Act of Hope

O my God,
trusting in Your infinite goodness and promises,
I hope to obtain pardon of my sins,
the help of Your grace,
and life everlasting,
through the merits of Jesus Christ,
my Lord and Redeemer. Amen.

Act of Love

O my God,
I love You above all things,
with my whole heart and soul,
because You are all-good
and worthy of all my love.
I love my neighbor as myself
for love of You.
I forgive all who have injured me,
and I ask pardon of all whom I have injured. Amen.

Act of Contrition

O my God,
I am heartily sorry for having offended You,
and I detest all my sins,

because I dread the loss of heaven
and the pains of hell,
but most of all because they offend You, my God,
Who are all-good and deserving of all my love.
I firmly resolve,
with the help of Your grace,
to confess my sins,
to do penance,
and to amend my life. Amen.

Blessing Before Meals

Bless us, O Lord, and these Your gifts
which we are about to receive
from Your bounty,
through Christ our Lord. Amen.

Thanksgiving After Meals

We give You thanks, Almighty God,
for these and all Your blessings;
You live and reign for ever and ever, Amen.

Hail, Holy Queen

Hail, Holy Queen, Mother of Mercy,
hail our life, our sweetness, and our hope!
To you do we cry, poor banished children of Eve!
To you do we send up our sighs;
mourning and weeping in this vale of tears!

Turn then, most gracious Advocate,
your eyes of mercy toward us;
and after this, our exile,
show unto us the blessed fruit of your womb, Jesus!
O clement, O loving, O sweet Virgin Mary!

Night Prayer

I adore You, my God,
and thank You for having created me,
for having made me a Christian

and preserved me this day.
I love You with all my heart
and I am sorry for having sinned against You,
because You are infinite Love and infinite Goodness.
Protect me during my rest
and may Your love be always with me. Amen.